Free Chicago

Free things to see and do in the Chicagoland area.

RIVERDALE PUBLIC LIBRARY
208 W. 144TH STREET
RIVERDALE, IL 60827
(708) 841-3311

By James V. Bilodeau

ISBN 978-0-9790227-3-9

Library of Congress Control Number: 2008921666

Printed in the U.S.A.

The author, staff, and publisher accepts no responsibility for loss due to errors, omissions, inaccuracies or inconsistencies incurred within. Readers are encouraged to call ahead, or visit the web-page of any attraction they choose for any information changes.

Cover design by James V. Bilodeau

Edited by James C. Hamilton

Layout by Amanda N. Huffman

Chicagoland Fun Fact (pg. 129) Contributed by Adrianne Curry

Contents

Introduction... 11

Science and Industry.. 19

    Argonne National Laboratory   21

    Herbert Trackman Planetarium   23

    McDonald's USA First Store Museum   24

    Chicago Mercantile Exchange   26

    John G. Shedd Aquarium   28

    The ABA Museum of Law   29

    The Museum of Science and Industry   30

    Adler Planetarium & Astronomy Museum   32

    Chicago Board of Trade   33

    Fermi National Accelerator Laboratory   35

    Chicago Architecture Foundation   37

History Museums...………..……………………….…...... 39

    Wilmette Historical Museum   41

    Isle A La Cache Museum   42

    DuSable Museum of African American History   43

    Elmhurst Historical Museum   44

    Kankakee County Museum   45

    Hawthorne Museum   48

    The Chicago History Museum   50

    The Oriental Institute   52

Bartlett History Museum   53

Lombard Historical Museum   54

West Chicago City Museum   55

Historical Sites.. 57

Jane Addams Hull-House Museum   59

Batavia Depot Museum   60

Glessner House Museum   62

Historic Pleasant Home   63

Joliet Iron Works Historic Site   64

William L. Gregg House Museum   65

Sheldon Peck Homestead   66

The Farmhouse Museum   67

Lisle Station Museum   68

Religious Sites.. 69

Conventual Franciscan Friars of Marytown   71

Baha'i House of Worship of North America   73

Rockefeller Memorial Chapel   75

The National Shrine of St. Therese   77

Billy Graham Center Museum   78

Art Galleries and Museums...................................... 81

The Art Institute of Chicago   83

Skokie Northshore Sculpture Park   85

Mary and Leigh Block Museum of Art   86

Intuit: The Center for Intuitive and Outsider Art   88

National Museum of Mexican Art   89

Elmhurst Art Museum   90

DePaul University Museum   91

The Renaissance Society   92

The Museum of Contemporary Art   93

Antioch Fine Arts Foundation Gallery   95

Union Street Gallery   96

Smith Museum of Stained Glass Windows   97

Illinois State Museum Chicago Gallery   98

American Toby Jug Museum   99

The Chicago Cultural Center   100

Hyde Park Art Center   102

Lizzardo Museum of Lapidary Art   103

The Arts Club of Chicago   104

Smart Museum of Art   105

Donald E. Stephens Museum of Hummels   106

The Museum of Contemporary Photography   108

Nature Days... 109

Notebaert Nature Museum   111

Sand Ridge Nature Center   113

Kline Creek Farm/Timber Ridge Forest Preserve   114

Spring Valley Nature Sanctuary   116

Lake Catherine Nature Center and Botanic Gardens   117

Fullersburg Woods   118

Phillips Park Zoo   119

Chicago Botanic Garden   120

Willowbrook Wildlife Center   121

Plum Creek Nature Center/Goodenow Grove   123

The Grove   125

The Lincoln Park Zoo   127

Bird Haven Greenhouse   129

Garfield Park Conservatory   130

Wagner Farm   132

Lincoln Park Conservatory   134

Uniquely Chicagoland.. 135

Marion E. Wade Center   137

Chicago Children's Museum   139

Elks National Veterans Memorial   141

Millennium Park   143

Balzekas Museum of Lithuanian Culture   145

Grant Park   146

Swedish American Museum Center   148

Harold Washington Library Center   149

The Newberry Library   152

The Jerry Springer Show   153

Chicago Bears Training Camp   155

Downers Grove Plowboys Vintage Baseball Club   157

Oprah Winfrey Show   159

Chicago Greeter Service   162

Appendix... 165

INTRODUCTION

Introduction

Even in this day and age of super corporations, world trade, stock market gambles, and a general preoccupation for wealth – many things are still free. Tourism today is a multi-billion dollar industry which is growing at a rapid pace. Mega-amusement parks, roadside attractions, and family adventures pop up across the countryside on a daily basis. Many states are latching onto the tourism industry in attempt to bring in additional revenue to tight state budgets. States such as: New Mexico, Maryland, Kentucky, and Illinois have been at the fore-front of this movement. With aggressive advertising, trade show promotion, and tax incentives, tourism has grown tremendously within these states. Most of the increase in the number of attractions are for-profit ventures, but even in the booming for profit tourism industry; there are many opportunities for free entertainment.

Reasons things are free

With all of the for-profit tourism ventures popping up, it may seem odd that there are places that still do not charge an admission fee. There are many reasons for this, and they are as varied as the attractions themselves. The one common theme, that all the free attractions have, is they all have a specific goal other than profit. Some things are free simply based on the mission of the attraction.

Churches are an example of this. Churches have the specific purpose of sharing their faith and traditions. Churches, especially Catholic churches, are commonly open most of the day and night for silent reflection and prayer. The churches in this book are known for the beauty of their design and decor and gladly welcome visitors who want to admire their beauty.

Zoos and gardens serve the purpose of preserving different species of animals and plants. Gardens and arboretums are commonly run by clubs whose members provide the labor for the upkeep of the flora. Many of these gardens serve as educational facilities and test gardens for new plant species and growing techniques.

Museums, both art and history, have a long tradition of being free to visitors. Recently a number of museums have started charging admission fees, although most just a few dollars. The majority of museums are still free, and this will probably remain the case for many years since most museums are run by universities and historical societies. These organizations have an interest in educating visitors about the history of their area, as well as building respect for the subject matter of the museum.

Government entities are well known for offering free attractions. Just as most attractions are free in Washington D.C., the same thing is true in the states. One purpose for governments offering free museums and activities is to allow the public to "see their tax dollars at work." Museums on military bases often serve as military recruitment tools. State capitol building tours foster pride and confidence the state government system. Fish hatchery tours show the government making effective use of tax dollars for the good of nature. Anytime politicians are involved there is an extensive effort to build good public relations with potential voters!

Much like the government, businesses also like to build good public relations. Unlike the government, businesses are trying to make a profit. Even with this motivation, businesses have seen the need in providing free recreational opportunities to their current and future customers. The trade tour, in which visitors get to see first hand the production of a product, has been an emerging attraction. Businesses find if they allow people to see their product being made it builds consumer confidence in the product itself. It is common for people to feel more connected to a product and become loyal repeat customers. Businesses take these tours very seriously and make sure that their tours are high quality, entertaining experiences. The trade tour also gives the visitor the impression that the company is "giving something back" to the community. Recently some businesses have started charging visitors for their tours. Many people think that this is a bad business practice, because it negates some of the positive public relations benefits of the tours.

How Free Things Stay in Business

One of the oldest business mantras is "Don't give away the store"! How can something stay in business if their sole purpose is not to charge for their service? Businesses which offer free trade tours obviously make a profit from the sale of their products, but what about the attractions with nothing to sell? The answer to this question is their ability to operate on a shoestring budget and creatively raise funds.

Grants

One major revenue stream for free attractions comes in the form of grants. Grants are blocks of money that are awarded to an entity based on its need, and the service that it provides to the public. Although most grants come from government entities, there are also a number of grants that are awarded by major corporations. Winning grants is not an easy task. An attraction wishing to apply for a grant must fill out the appropriate applications, and must be able to convince the issuer of the grant of their worthiness to receive the grant. The competition for grants is very competitive so attractions end up getting very few of the awards that they apply for.

Although almost all free attractions depend on grant money to make ends meet, some do have the luxury of having a regular budget. Some attractions, mostly of a historical nature, are actually provided a portion of their operating budget from local city and county governments. To get this type of funding the organization's purpose is usually to display artifacts and information about the history of the local town or county. Government attractions will usually be mostly funded through a regular annual budget. Whether the organization is partially funded, or completely funded through government dollars, the amount of funding given is almost always based on the number of people the attraction serves. Most of the time an attraction will use a guest book to keep track of the number they serve. If you see a guest book please fill it out. If you don't your favorite attraction may lose important funding.

Memberships

One innovative way free attractions have found to increase funding is through the sale of memberships. History museums have done this for some time by offering memberships to a historical society that oversees the museum's operation. Although selling memberships is not a common practice among businesses offering trade tours – the sale of memberships is becoming a regular occurrence. For their membership fee the member usually is entitled to receive a newsletter and gets invited to various private functions and social gatherings. The members usually consist of high profile community and business leaders, or people who want to be. Memberships are often bought for the status and networking opportunities among business people. Since membership sales have been such an effective money generating tool, some "for-profit" organizations have also started membership programs.

Donation Box

In addition to innovative membership programs, free attractions also rely on the most basic methods of fund raising. The most basic form of fundraising is the traditional donation box. Nowadays the donation box occupies a prominent place near the attraction's entrance and is often decorated to be easily noticed. The humble donation box still is one of the most effective means of fundraising, as well as the least intrusive. Sometimes an attendant will make a request for a donation, but this is a very rare occurrence.

Gift Shops

The traditional gift shop has been a stalwart in the fundraising process. Many gift shops today are stocked with high quality items that pertain to the attraction itself. Gone are the days of the tacky t-shirt and plastic cups. The increasing popularity of the internet has led to the creation of online gift shops which offer the same high quality souvenirs as the gift shop on location. The concept of the gift shop remains the same; profits generated are used for the attraction's upkeep.

Volunteers

For a free attraction to stay open more than money is needed, a motivated workforce is essential. This motivated workforce almost always works for free. In almost all cases an attraction will have just one or two employees that draw a salary of any kind. If an employee draws a salary it is usually one that is lower then they could normally get with their level of education and experience. The highest level staff person at an attraction can commonly be found filling out grant applications, seeking donations, sweeping the floor, giving tours, and cleaning bathrooms. Most of these staffers do their job for the love of what they do. Most of the additional workers are unpaid volunteers.

Donations

In this book, free means free. Every effort has been made to weed out the "free" attractions from the ones with a specific "suggested donation." It is very typical in the Chicagoland area for many attractions to offer limited free admission days. Where possible the free days are listed at the top of each attraction's page in this book. If you wish to donate to any attraction you see, great! Donate in the amount you feel is fair based on your enjoyment. If you choose to buy souvenirs on your trip, please consider shopping at a free attraction's gift shop. If you feel like donating, and don't see a donation box, just ask any staffer and they will be more then happy to accept your gift.

The Cost of Entertainment

There is no doubt that things are not as affordable as they used to be. The hard earned dollar simply doesn't go as far. In addition to ever rising fuel costs, admission fees to pretty much every type of event or attraction has shot up in recent years. It is typical for a museum or aquarium to charge $9.00 or $15.00 per person. With the typical family of five that would be $45-70 just to get in the door. If the family wants to go to an amusement park, the gate entrance can cost as much as $20 to $25 per person. This would mean a family of five will spend over $125 for a day of fun, not including food, gas, and parking!

Why this book

When I was growing up in rural Southern Kentucky our family would hardly be considered wealthy. We had a very modest home sitting on a small farm. We grew our own vegetables and raised chickens for eggs and livestock for meat. Because of very shrewd decision making by my parents we never missed a meal, but there were very few extras. We had no cable, no fancy sneakers, no internet, and my parents drove used cars. The cloths were hand me downs, yard sale deals, and some were even homemade! Needless to say our entertainment budget was pretty much non-existent. Our entertainment consisted of visiting state parks, historic sites, and other – you guessed it – free attractions! Most of the things we visited we heard about through the grapevine. Today with the internet and books like *Free Chicago* it is easier to find many opportunities for free entertainment ideas.

SCIENCE AND INDUSTRY

Argonne National Laboratory

9700 South Cass Avenue

Argonne, IL 60439

630-252-2000

Free Admission Days: Always Free

The beginnings of the Argonne National Laboratory actually started in 1942, when a group of scientists led by Enrico Fermi created the first ever controlled nuclear chain reaction at the University of Chicago. The University of Chicago Metallurgical Laboratory was a part of the ultra secret Manhattan Project of World War II. Because of this accomplishment, the Argonne National Laboratory was chartered in 1946 with the mission of developing nuclear reactors for peaceful purposes.

It is ironic that, despite its beginnings, the Argonne National Laboratory is not (and has never been) a weapons laboratory. Today the mission of the Argonne facility has expanded. The laboratory currently engages in various research projects including: experimental work in various scientific disciplines, the design of new research facilities, environmental management, national security, and the search for clean sustainable energy sources.

The success of the Argonne National Laboratory has always been the people who work in the facility. Today the facility employs almost 3,000 people, with about 30% of those people holding Doctoral degrees. In its history, Argonne has been home to three Nobel Prize winners in the field of physics, the most notable winner being Maria Goeppert Mayer who won for her research pertaining to the shell model of the atomic nucleus.

The grounds of the laboratory are actually very surprising consisting of 1,500 acres of woodlands. These woodlands are home to two distinct species of deer: whitetail deer (commonly referred to as brown deer by locals) and white deer. It is commonly thought that the white deer are the result of experimentation at Argonne. The reason for the deer is much less sinister though. The deer are the result of a gift to local hot dog tycoon Gustav Freund from Chicago clothier Maurice L. Rothchild.

After the white deer started eating Freund's orchards the local game warden set out to destroy the deer herd. Fortunately for the species the warden missed two deer, thus about 30 of the rare species live on the facility's grounds today. Surprisingly the white deer and brown deer co-exist peacefully and do not compete for food, nor do they interbreed.

In addition to the deer, visitors to the Argonne National Laboratory have the opportunity to see many other unique things. Tours are offered on Saturday morning and afternoon. Reservations are required and may be set up by calling the reservation line at (630) 252-5562. Visitors who wish to take the tour must be at least 16 years old. Tours normally begin at 9:00 a.m. and 1:00 p.m. and last about two and a half hours.

Chicagoland Fun Fact

The University of Chicago was established in 1892. The initial enrollment at the school consisted of 594 students. Amazingly the school had 103 faculty members resulting in student to faculty ratio of only 1 faculty member per 5.7 students, much lower than today's national average of 1 faculty member to 15.0 students.

Herbert Trackman Planetarium

1215 Houbolt Road

Joliet, IL 60431

815-280-6682

www.jjc.cc.il.us/Planetarium

Free Admission Days: Always Free

The Herbert Trackman Planetarium is located at the oldest public community college in America. Founded in 1901, Joliet Junior College (JCC) was organized as an educational experiment. The thought behind the experiment was to organize an educational program which would be the equivalent of the first two years at a typical four year university. The students of the school would be able to get a first class education while being able to remain in their community as long as possible. The Joliet Junior College experiment would later serve as an inspiration to future community colleges throughout the U.S.

Today over 31,000 students take classes at JCC. Astronomy is very popular at JCC due to the planetarium. The planetarium, with its state of the art equipment, is able to put on a variety of educational and entertaining programs. Multi-media equipment, video projection capabilities, and the Spitz System 512 projector all allow for a top quality programming schedule. The planetarium puts on a variety of shows dealing with different areas of astronomy. Some shows focus on the planets, while others focus more on the stars and constellations. Details about specific shows can be found on the planetarium's web-site.

The planetarium has public shows on Tuesdays and Thursdays. The Tuesday show, which starts at 7:30 p.m., is geared toward audiences of all ages. The show on Thursday, which starts at 6:30 p.m., is geared more toward children. Each of the shows lasts from 35 to 45 minutes. It is advised that visitors arrive early since the seats fill up quickly.

McDonald's USA First Store Museum

400 North Lee Street

Des Plaines, IL 60016

847-297-5022

http://www.mcdonalds.com/corp/about/museum_info.html

Free Admission Days: Always Free

On April 15, 1955, American fast food history would be changed forever. On that date Ray Kroc opened what would be the first of thousands of McDonald's restaurants to span the country and the world. The idea for McDonald's came to Kroc when he learned of two California brothers who had purchased eight multi-mixers from Kroc's employer. Curious Kroc ventured to California to see the restaurant required the use of so many mixers. What Kroc discovered was a new type of restaurant. Walk-up service and a limited menu greeted the customer. Although the menu was small the food was fast!

Originally Kroc had the idea to get the McDonald brothers to open more restaurants-for which he would be more than happy to sell them eight multi-mixers apiece. When all was said and done the person who ended up opening the additional restaurants was Kroc himself. After his success with his first restaurant, Kroc gained the franchise rights from the McDonald brothers and never looked back.

Over the years Kroc continued the innovative spirit of the original McDonald brothers with several innovations of his own. In 1963, Kroc brought out the friendly Ronald McDonald character to appeal to children. 1968 brought about the invention of the Big Mac, and in 1971 McDonald's went international, opening a restaurant in Australia. More innovations followed including the invention of the Egg McMuffin in 1973, and the legendary Happy Meal in 1979.

Throughout the years McDonald's international presence grew to include more countries than just Australia. Britain's first restaurant, in 1974, became the company's 3,000 restaurant worldwide. McDonald's restaurants also played a role in end of the Cold War with the opening of a Moscow restaurant in 1990.

One of the things that McDonald's is most famous for is their charity work. McDonald's founded the Ronald McDonald House in 1974 in order to provide the families of terminally ill children a place to stay during their child's long periods of treatment. The first Ronald McDonald house opened in Philadelphia with the help of former Philadelphia Eagles football player Fred Hill. Today over 250 Ronald McDonald Houses are in existence. In addition to the houses, there are many foundations which help to distribute funds to worthy organizations.

At the McDonald's USA First Store Museum visitors get to see first hand a meticulous recreation of the original 1955 store. The ground floor contains much of the original equipment "manned" by mannequins dressed in the typical 1955 McDonald's uniform. Downstairs there is a gallery which is dedicated to the images and memorabilia of the McDonald's company through the years. At the museum there is also a short video presentation on the history of the company.

Across the street there is a modern working McDonald's restaurant with additional artifacts decorating the dining area. The museum is open between Memorial Day and Labor Day. Hours vary so visitors are encouraged to call ahead.

Chicagoland Fun Fact

Amazingly, one out of every eight American workers has been employed by McDonald's at some point in their lives, the author of this book included!

Chicago Mercantile Exchange

20 South Wacker Drive

Chicago, IL 60606

312-930-1000

www.cme.com

Free Admission Days: Always Free

The Chicago Mercantile Exchange (CME) was founded in 1898 as an off shoot of the Chicago Board of Trade. Originally known as the Chicago Butter and Egg Board, the CME reorganized in 1919 and began trading in futures. From that time the CME has been a leader in the use of technology in its trading business. Like the Chicago Board of Trade, the CME makes use of open outcry trading. In open outcry trading many simultaneous "auctions" take place on a crowded trading area known as "the pit". Utilizing different colored jackets, hand signals, and the raising and lowering of the pit areas, trading goes by relatively smoothly, with a minimum of miscommunication.

What has set the CME apart from other exchanges is its adoption of technology to facilitate trading. Today over two-thirds of all trading is done electronically. The CME has developed a system called CME Globex to facilitate trading action. The success of the CME Globex system has pushed many exchanges around the world to shift to a more electronic system. Exchanges from the New York Stock Exchange to the Chinese Stock Exchange have embraced technology to better handle trading functions. It is thought that in the near future open outcry trading will go the way of the dinosaur.

In 2006, the CME purchased the Chicago Board of Trade, reuniting the two organizations once again. The $8 billion dollar purchase has created the world's dominant futures market.

At the CME visitor's center guests can learn more about the history of the CME, commonly known as "The Merc". Exhibits detailing the history and activities of the CME are present. Information about the merger and the new position the Chicago exchanges hold in world trading is also illustrated. Visitors are encouraged to call ahead for hours and additional information.

Chicagoland Fun Fact

Chicago hired its first female police officer in 1893. Even though Mary Evans was be the first female officer, she did not actually get a uniform. Female officers were finally issued uniforms in 1956.

John G. Shedd Aquarium

1200 South Lake Shore Drive

Chicago, IL 60605

312-939-2438

www.sheddaquarium.org

Free Admission Days: Various

In 1924 $2 million was donated by John Groves Shedd for the construction of what would then be the largest indoor aquarium in the world. Shedd envisioned a place where visitors would be able to see a wide variety of aquatic life. What resulted from Shedd's donation was the first inland aquarium to feature both freshwater and saltwater species. The aquarium building was designed in the beaux-arts style by architectural firm Graham, Anderson, Probst, & White. The building is unique in the fact that there are Greek elements added to better match the aquarium to the nearby Field Museum.

Throughout the years the aquarium had added a variety of facilities and species. Everything from sharks to river otters call the aquarium home. The sheer variety of species keeps visitors coming back time and time again. Many activities are available at the aquarium including presentation, a "4-D" theatre, and restaurants. The aquarium entertains about 2 million visitors per year, making it one of the most visited sites in the city.

The aquarium keeps hours of 9:00 a.m. to 5:00 p.m., Monday through Friday. On weekends the aquarium stays open until 6:00 p.m. On free days visitors will get a general admission ticket. There will be an extra charge for the Oceanarium and Wild Reef areas. Currently the aquarium offers free admission everyday to active military, teachers, and Chicago's police officers and firefighters.

The ABA Museum of Law

321 North Clark Street

Chicago, IL 60610

312-988-6222

www.abanet.org/museum/

Free Admission Days: Always Free

Before the founding of the American Bar Association (ABA) in 1878, the legal profession was very unorganized and unregulated. Most lawyers were trained through their work as apprentices under more experienced lawyers. Some lawyers had even less formal training and simply learned their craft through books and self-study. Because of the growing complexity of the American legal system, a group of 100 lawyers representing 21 states gathered in Saratoga Springs, New York to found the ABA.

Today the ABA has a membership of over 400,000 legal professionals from all over the world. The ABA today works to serve the legal industry as the leader in the training of judges, lawyers, and other legal professionals. As the leader in legal training, the ABA also serves as the accreditation organization for law schools. The ABA also seeks to work to improve the legal system for all those who need to use it.

As part of its public mission, the ABA established the Museum of Law in 1996. From its early days the 4,300 square foot museum has educated the public on the origins of the American legal system, as well as its characters and high profile cases. Since the museum changes its exhibits periodically, the museum is a place that can be enjoyed year after year. The museum, which is located on the lower level of the ABA headquarters, is open Monday through Friday from 10:00 a.m. to 4:00 p.m.

The Museum of Science and Industry

57th Street and Lake Shore Drive

Chicago, IL 60637

773-684-1414

www.msichicago.org

Free Admission Days: Varies

In 1911 Julius Rosenwald, the Chairman of Sears Roebuck & Company, made a trip to visit the Deutches Museum in Munich, Germany. After having the chance to view Deutches, Rosenwald became inspired to create a similar museum in Chicago. The museum he envisioned would be filled with interactive exhibits rather than exhibits which are simply viewed. Rosenwald wanted to create a museum which also celebrated the industrial spirit of America and Chicago.

In 1933, Rosenwald's dream became a reality with the opening of the Museum of Science and Industry. Throughout the years the museum has entertained nearly 160 million visitors of all ages. The museum, which contains over 800 exhibits, contains everything from entire airplanes to sub marines. The 350,000 square foot museum also contains over 2000 interactive items which allow visitors to learn first hand about a variety of topics.

The museum contains a variety of one-of-a-kind objects that visitors can see, and in some cases get in or climb aboard. Some of the unique items include a Boeing 747, a coal mine elevator, a WWII German submarine, and even a 16 foot artificial heart. One of the most unique exhibits is the 3,500 square foot model railroad. This model railroad is one of the largest in the world. The railroad exhibit serves to tell the story of rail travel between Chicago and Seattle.

For those who like airplanes, the museum offers much to see. In addition to the 747, the museum is also home to a wide variety of flying machines. The "air fleet" of the museum contains a Piccard Stratosphere Gondola, the Texaco Racer Plane, and a WWII Spitfire fighter plane.

Some out of this world aircraft are even present. These include the Apollo 8 Spacecraft, The Mercury 7 craft, and a Lunar Module Trainer.

The museum is also filled with a variety of cars and boats. One of the most notable cars is the 1912 Sears Motor Buggy antique car. This car could actually be ordered direct through the Sears catalog! The museum also contains an impressive collection of 50 model ships. These models illustrate the art of shipbuilding from about 5,000 years ago to the mid 20th century.

The past days of trade and commerce are also illustrated at the museum. The best example of this is the *Yesterday's Main Street* exhibit. This exhibit is a complete reproduction of a typical early 1900's main street. The street is complete with a cobblestone road, fire hydrants, light fixtures, and even several shops. A typical grocery store, restaurant, post office, druggist, law office, and clothing store are all represented. The thing that makes this street interesting is there are actually two working businesses on the street. You can visit Finnigan's Ice Cream Parlor and have a frozen treat, or you could visit The Nickelodeon Cinema and check out a short film for a nickel.

Along with the industrial side, the science side of the museum has a lot for visitors to enjoy. Many exhibits are presented which illustrate the workings of the human body. *AIDS: The War Within* tells the story of the history behind AIDS and the efforts being made to combat the deadly disease. *Body Worlds* is practically a museum unto itself. This exhibit contains the 16 foot heart as well as other exhibits which illustrate the inner workings of the human body. Displays pertaining to the human life cycle are present. There are also cadavers which are exposed to allow visitors to see the real organs of the human body. Please note that the *Body Worlds* exhibit does contain real cadavers and other "anatomically correct" displays so much care should be taken before deciding if you want to take your kids to this section of the museum. It is important to note that even on the free days, some of the exhibits such as *Body Worlds* charge an additional fee. The museum also has a theatre and gift shop.

Adler Planetarium & Astronomy Museum

1300 South Lake Shore Drive

Chicago, IL 60605

312-922-STAR

www.adlerplanetarium.org

Free Admission Days: Varies

Built in 1930, the Adler Planetarium & Astronomy Museum was the product of Chicago businessman Max Adler. Adler had learned of the device invented by Dr. Walther Bauersfeld in 1923 which was able to accurately create a representation of the nighttime sky on a domed ceiling. After Adler, his wife, and architect Ernest Grunsfeld traveled to Germany to see the device in person, Alder fronted all of the required funds to construct what would become the first modern planetarium located in the Western Hemisphere. In addition to the planetarium, Alder also contributed the historical artifacts which would form the foundation for one of the most complete collections of astronomy equipment in the world.

Today the Adler Planetarium & Astronomy Museum still remains one of the most advanced planetariums in the world. This continued quality has been due to many upgrades that the facility has received through the years. To the original structure has been added a second planetarium, a special effects escalator, expanded museum, observatory, and gift shops. The museum at Adler contains artifacts from astronomy dating back to the 12th century. Over 35,000 feet is dedicated to exhibits in the museum portion of the complex. Most of the exhibits at the facility are geared toward children, as well as the planetarium shows. The hours for the facility normally run from 9:30 a.m. to 4:30 p.m. daily.

Chicago Board of Trade

141 West Jackson Boulevard

Chicago, IL 60604

312-435-3500

www.cbot.com

Free Admission Days: Always Free

In 1848, the Chicago Board of Trade was established to serve as a trading place for futures contracts. In 1930, the Chicago Board of Trade moved into its present location on West Jackson Boulevard. The 605 foot tall building was designed by the architectural firm of Holabird & Root in the art deco style. At the time the building was the tallest in Chicago. More impressively the building retained that distinction all the way up until 1965 when it was finally eclipsed in height by the Richard J. Daley Center. Interestingly, because of the building's height, the statute at its peak is faceless. The statue of the goddess Ceres was sculpted by John Storrs. Storrs felt that the building was so tall that nobody would be able to see the detail of his statue's face anyway.

As impressive as the Chicago Board of Trade is on the outside, inside is where the true action is located. Daily over 3,600 agents combine through on the floor trading and electronic trading to move close to 2 million contracts per business day. So high is the trading volume that it is common for the Board of Trade to exchange over 450 million contracts annually. Recently the Chicago Board of Trade merged with the Chicago Mercantile Exchange. This merger has created the world's largest commodities trading market.

At the Chicago Board of Trade visitors can experience the excitement and history of the trading floor through the first floor visitor's center. The visitor's center has streaming video, artifacts, brochures, and exhibits. The exhibits do a good job illustrating the history behind the Chicago Board of Trade, and the nuances of what happens on the trading floor.

The visitor's center at the Chicago Board of Trade is open from 8:00 a.m. to 4:00 p.m., Monday through Friday. The Board of Trade is closed on all holidays.

Chicagoland Fun Fact

In 1885, the first major automobile race held in the United States was a point to point race from Chicago to Evanston, Illinois. J. Frank Duryea was victorious that day with a blazing average speed of 7.3 miles per hour.

Fermi National Accelerator Laboratory

Wilson and Kirk Roads

Batavia, IL 60510

630-840-3351

www.fnal.gov

Free Admission Days: Always Free

For the last 40 years the Fermi National Accelerator Laboratory has served the United States as the premier facility for the study of high energy physics. The laboratory is operated under the guidance of the U.S. Department of Energy and enjoys an annual budget in excess of $275 million. Unlike a lot of government projects, the Fermi National Accelerator Laboratory was actually constructed for $7 million less than was appropriated. The total cost of construction in 1967 was $243 million. Construction of the four mile Tevatron (a particle accelerator) was completed in 1982 at a cost of $120 million.

All of the accelerators, labs, and detectors set on the facility's 6800 acres. One unique feature of the facility is its dual use as a scientific facility and a nature preserve. The acreage of the facility is home to many natural features and animals. The most popular of the animals at the facility are the herd of 60 buffalo which are available for viewing from mid-October to mid-April. Many other animals such as birds, raccoons, butterflies, and fish make their home at Fermi. Fermi has ponds open for fishing (Illinois fishing license required) and trails for bicycling. Horses and dogs are even allowed at Fermi (dogs must be leashed).

For the true science enthusiast a trip to Fermi will be a tremendously entertaining experience. The Lederman Science Center is home to many hands on exhibits dealing with all areas of physics. The exhibits are aimed at students, but many adults are intrigued and challenged by the exhibits (it is physics after all). Occasionally there is an interesting program called *Ask a Scientist*. This program allows guests to have all of their burning physics questions answered by the experts. On a monthly basis Fermi offers visitors a chance to see some of the areas not usually seen by the general public. The behind-the-scenes tour offers visitors the chance to see the magnet factory, neutrino experiments, and the accelerator complex. Visitors interested in the full tour are encouraged to call ahead for dates and times.

Having something for everybody, Fermi even has things for art lovers. The complex is home to many distinct pieces of artwork. Sculptures like the Mobius Strip, Broken Symmetry, and Tractricious all add beauty and thought to the facility. In addition to the art, the paint schemes of the buildings help to brighten things up at the lab. Visitors to the Fermi National Accelerator Laboratory are strongly advised to call ahead or visit the web-site due to today's security concerns. Fermi is accessible through one of the two security checkpoints located on Pine Street and Batavia Road. The hours for the facility grounds are 8:00 a.m. to 6:00 p.m. from mid-October to mid-April. During the rest of the year the grounds stay open until 8:00 p.m. The hours for the Lederman Science Center are 8:30 a.m. to 4:30 p.m., Monday through Friday. The Lederman Science Center is also open Saturday from 9:00 a.m. until 3:00 p.m.

Chicagoland Fun Fact

In 2007 Batavia was named by *Business Week* as one of the "50 best places to raise kids".

Chicago Architecture Foundation

224 South Michigan Avenue

Chicago, IL 60604

312-922-3432 ext. 240

www.architecture.org

Free Admission Days: Always Free

In 1960, Chicago was about to lose one of its most valuable landmarks. The John J. Glessner House had suffered from years of neglect and was slated for demolition. The house was important to the history of Chicago due to its former role as the home of John J. Glessner, an executive with the International Harvester Company. In order to save the house a group of community leaders formed the Chicago Architecture Foundation to aid in the effort. After the house was saved, and listed in the National Register of Historic Places in 1970, the foundation decided to continue its mission of preserving the architectural history of the city.

Today the Chicago Architecture Foundation serves the city, and its visitors, as the focal point for the education of Chicago's rich architectural heritage. The main tool offered to the public is the foundation's ArcelorMittal CitySpace Gallery. The free gallery is supported by the Illinois Department of Commerce and Economic Opportunity and ArcelorMittal and serves as a starting point for those who want to learn about the city and its buildings. The gallery contains photos, videos, models, and displays which depict the history and people behind Chicago's impressive buildings. One of the most interesting and useful exhibits is a replica model of downtown Chicago and all of its major buildings.

The ArcelorMittal CitySpace Gallery is open to the public from 9:30 a.m. to 5:00 p.m. every day.

HISTORY MUSEUMS

Wilmette Historical Museum

609 Ridge Road

Wilmette, IL 60091

847-853-7666

www.wilmettehistory.org

Free Admission Days: Always Free

For over 50 years the Wilmette Historical Museum has sought to preserve the history of Wilmette and its relationship to the Chicagoland area. From its meager start in the Village Hall's basement, the museum has grown and moved many times during its history. The current location of the museum opened in 1995 after a lengthy restoration effort. The historical 1896 Gross Point Village Hall was saved from commercial development by a motivated group of community leaders and elected officials. Since its purchase the building has been renovated and expanded to increase its usefulness to the museum, community, and the Wilmette Historical Society.

Throughout time the museum has gathered a variety of artifacts including arrowheads, wood samples, and even a foot from an Egyptian mummy. Today exhibits pertaining to Wilmette and the surrounding area dominate the museum's collection. The museum is loaded with photographs, murals, paintings, tools, clothing, and furnishings. Special attention is paid to the dramatic events which helped shape the community, such as the devastating 1920 Palm Sunday Tornado.

A children's favorite at the Wilmette Historical Museum is the Historic Gross Point Jail exhibit. The exhibit recreates the old four cell jail that housed the roughest scofflaws of Wilmette and Gross Point. Police equipment including badges, hats, and billy clubs are included in the jail exhibit.

The Wilmette Historical Museum keeps hours of 1:00 p.m. to 4:30 p.m., Sunday through Thursday.

Isle A La Cache Museum

501 East Romeo Road

Romeoville, IL 60446

815-886-1467

www.fpdwc.org/isle.cfm

Free Admission Days: Always Free

During the 1700's Isle a la Cache served French fur trappers and traders as a storage point for beaver pelts which were harvested from the river. The European fashion of the day made the trade of beaver pelts quite lucrative. The pelts were a popular material for hats worn by Europe's social elite. In addition to hoity toity Europeans, the Native Americans of the region also very much enjoyed wearing the beaver furs, but more out of necessity than fashion.

Legend has it, since the area was so rough, the French fur traders would hide their equipment on the island as they traveled the region tending to their traps. Isle a la Cache became the unofficial name of the island, translated as "Island of the Hiding Place". What is not hidden today is the museum which is dedicated to the history of the area, its trappers, and its native cultures.

Isle a la Cache Museum, renovated in 2007, contains a large "cache" of artifacts detailing the history of the island. Weapons and clothing are preserved at the museum in Plexiglas cases. Fortunately for visitors many of the exhibits are interactive. Authentic canoes make their home at the museum, as well as a wigwam. Items which were traded between the French explorers and the Native Americans are also on display. One of the favorite items on display is a stuffed beaver. Ever popular with the children, the museum actually encourages kids and adults to touch the beaver.

The Isle a la Cache Museum is open from 10:00 a.m. to 4:00 p.m., Tuesday through Saturday. On Sundays the museum is open from noon until 4:00 p.m.

DuSable Museum of African American History

740 East 56th Place

Chicago, IL 60637

773-947-0600

www.dusablemuseum.org

Free Admission Days: Sundays Free

In 1961, a group of people came together to combat what they saw as a lack of representation of black art and culture in the area's educational institutions. What resulted was the Ebony Museum of Negro History and Art. The museum served as the first repository of black culture and historical artifacts in the city of Chicago. The first decade of the museum was spent in John Griffin's former home, which would later serve as a railroad worker boarding home.

In 1968, the museum was renamed after Chicago's first permanent settler Jean Baptist Pointe DuSable. Shortly after the renaming of the museum it was able to acquire a new location in the former parks administration building. This museum became the primary memorial to DuSable and his importance to the city's history. Over the years the building has been expanded adding a new wing, theatre, museum store, and cutting edge security and computer systems.

At the DuSable Museum visitors will have the chance to learn about Chicago's first permanent setter, as well as all aspects of African-American history and culture. The museum hosts various traveling exhibits throughout the year pertaining to black history and events. The museum is open Tuesday through Saturday from 10:00 a.m. to 5:00 p.m. On Sundays the museum keeps hours of noon to 5:00 p.m.

Elmhurst Historical Museum

120 East Park Avenue

Elmhurst, IL 60126

630-833-1457

www.elmhurst.org

Free Admission Days: Always Free

Since 1957, the city of Elmhurst has operated a museum dedicated to the history of the town. The Elmhurst Historical Museum is located in the old Glos Mansion. The 1892 mansion was built by Henry L. Glos, famous for being the first Village President of Elmhurst. Since 1939, the city has owned the mansion and has used it for various purposes. During its history the mansion has been a home, a traffic court, the city hall, and presently a museum. Since the home has been renovated at least three times, very little is known about the original floor plan. Today the mansion looks very little like a home, but at least the current layout serves the museum's purpose well.

The museum is home to many different artifacts and research tools. All of the artifacts contained in the museum are local to the area. Perhaps the most interesting collection of artifacts is the quilt collection. The quilt collection consists of 32 different quilts crafted between 1860 and 2003. The collection combines pieces which were owned by 25 different local families. Another noteworthy collection is the Christmas ornament collection. The collection of ornaments is made up of over 450 ornaments from the last 100 years. Within the large collection of ornaments is a group of 54 Dresden ornaments. The ornaments pay tribute to the influence of German culture to the area.

The museum also contains a variety of church records, deeds, newspapers, books, and maps pertaining to Elmhurst and its people. The museum is open to the public Tuesday through Sunday between 1:00 p.m. until 5:00 p.m. The research area is open during the same hours, although appointments are encouraged.

Kankakee County Museum
801 South Eighth Avenue
Kankakee, IL 60901
815-932-5279
www.kankakeecountymuseum.com
Free Admission Days: Always Free

For over 100 years the Kankakee County Historical Society has served the community as a collecting force for artifacts which depict the long history of Kankakee County. From its early days to the present the society has grown in size and in mission. The Kankakee County Historical Society was born in 1906 when the "Old Settler's Club" chose to organize themselves in an effort to preserve the county's history. A few years after formally organizing, the society opened its first museum using space donated by the local high school. From 1912 to 1936, the collection resided at the school before moving to the courthouse. A few years (and a move or two later) the museum collection would gain a permanent home.

In 1948, the current museum location opened to the public. Over the years, as the collection has grown, so has the facility. 1992 brought about the most recent expansion. Now officially a museum complex, the grounds include the museum, the Taylor School House, and the Dr. A.L. Small House. The three buildings enable visitors to be immersed in the history of the county, what it was like to learn there, and what it was like to live there.

The museum itself is home to several permanent-as well as temporary-exhibits. Permanent exhibits, such as *The Story of Kankakee County* explore the county's founding, early settlers, businesses, and the effect of the environment on the growth of the new area.

One distinction the area has is the fact that it is the only county in Illinois to have three native born Illinois Governors. The *Three Governor's*

Gallery details the lives and service of Governors Lennington Small, Samuel Shapiro, and George Ryan. The exhibit is complete with political memorabilia from their campaigns, mementos from their time of service, and pieces of furniture that were used during their time in office.

Kankakee County Native American Archeology is another permanent exhibit at the museum. Native American life is detailed for all to see. The exhibit contains many artifacts which were found in the immediate area. Over the years many exhibitions have unearthed tools, jewelry, and other treasures. The exhibit focuses on the interaction between the native people and the land prior to the introduction of European settlers.

The final permanent exhibit is the *Sculpture of George Grey Barnard* exhibit. The Barnard Exhibit contains 30 of Barnard's best sculptures. As a master sculptor Barnard created many pieces including a bust of Abraham Lincoln. Two pieces in the museum were intended to be part of a "peace arch" which he had planned to erect in New York City after WWI.

Many temporary exhibits inhabit the museum. For the most part the exhibits pertain to Kankakee County and its history. Annually the museum hosts the County Art League's annual art show.

Outside the main building the history lesson continues at the Taylor School House. In 1976 the building, which was originally constructed in 1904, was moved to the museum complex. In its day the schoolhouse was the learning place for grades one through eight. Amazingly the one room school was used all the up to 1948, without electricity!

The former home of the area's first Governor is also located at the complex. The Dr. A.L. Small House, allows visitors to see how an upper middle class family lived in the late 1800's and early 1900's. Governor Lennington Small was actually born in the house. The most amazing thing about the home is its authenticity. Today over 80% of the artifacts in the home are original items which were actually used by the Small family. Today the downstairs of the home is open to visitors and features the art collection of Susanne Smart. Susanne Smart was an accomplished artist who even traveled to Paris to study with Claude Monet.

The Kankakee County Museum is open from 10:00 a.m. to 4:00 p.m., Tuesday through Friday. On Sunday the museum keeps hours of 11:00 a.m. to 4:00 p.m. For those in a shopping mood there is a museum store which stocks all sorts of historical items and books.

Chicagoland Fun Fact

Sherb Noble, who would go on to found the ice cream chain Dairy Queen, actually opened his first ice cream shop in Kankakee (Sherb's). The first ice cream shop to carry the Dairy Queen name was opened by Sherb in Joliet.

Hawthorne Museum

Morton College

3801 South Central Avenue

Cicero, IL 60804

708-656-8000

www.morton.edu/museum

Free Admission Days: Always Free

From 1908 until 1983, the Hawthorne Works Manufacturing plant employed thousands of workers who produced the products which would change the way people communicated and experienced technology. Organized much like a small city, rather than simply a factory, the facility employed between 25,000 and 45,000 employees at any one time. The plant operated much like a small city complete with its own fire department, hospital, gymnasium, brass band, and running track. In addition to the production of technological marvels, the Hawthorne plant was the site of some ground breaking research in industrial psychology.

The research began when the industrial engineers at the plant wanted to find the optimal lighting levels in the plant. They thought the correct lighting levels would boost the worker's productivity. After several trials the engineers were surprised to find out that there was not a single lighting level which was best for boosting productivity. What the engineers found was any time they changed the lighting level the workers would increase their productivity for a period of time. The pattern remained true regardless if the engineers increased the light or reduced the light. Simply changing the lighting levels brought about positive results.

These initial experiments caught the eye of Harvard professor Elton Mayo. Mayo decided to run a variety of experiments at the plant testing the effect of various changes in the employee's routines. For five years the experiments continued and much knowledge was gained in the field of human behavior and human reaction to change. Because of these experiments innovations such as cross-training, cell groups, and incentive programs have been developed as motivational tools for industrial workers. These experiments and their results are standard learning material for college level instruction in the fields of Psychology and Manufacturing Management.

Today the Hawthorne Works Museum serves to preserve the history of the factory and the experiments which were preformed there. The Museum is open 10:00 a.m. to 2:00 p.m., Monday through Saturday.

Chicagoland Fun Fact

According to 2000 U.S. census figures over 43.6% of Cicero, Illinois residents were born in a foreign country.

The Chicago History Museum

1601 North Clark Street

Chicago, IL 60614

312-642-4600

www.chicagohistory.org

Free Admission Days: Mondays Free

Since 1851, the Chicago History Museum has served the Chicagoland
area as a focal point for the history of the city. The museums' early days
were spent telling the story of the transformation of Chicago from a
small frontier trading post to a major U.S. city. Unfortunately the
museum became a victim of the Great Fire of 1871, losing the vast
majority of its early artifacts. Among the early artifacts lost was an
original copy of the Emancipation Proclamation signed by President
Abraham Lincoln. Fortunately, the Chicago Historical Society was not
deterred in its mission, and the museum soon began to grow again.

Over the next 60 or so years the museum changed locations and rebuilt
their collection. In 1932, the museum moved into their new, and
reportedly fireproof, building. The new structure was designed in the
Georgian colonial style by architectural firm Graham, Anderson, Probst,
& White. Over the years the museum has undergone several
renovations. During the 70's and 80's the museum doubled in size due
to several construction efforts. The most recent renovation came in
2006 when upwards of 75% of the structure was updated.

Today the renovated museum serves to tell the history of Chicago, from
its founding to the present day. Many unique, and sometimes large,
artifacts currently make their home at the museum. One of the largest
artifacts at the museum is the CTA 1. The CTA 1 is the first passenger
car used for the Chicago "L" system. The CTA 1 car was used to
transport passengers during the World's Colombian Exposition. The
CTA 1 car also joins the Pioneer which served Chicago as its first
locomotive. The featuring of these two fine rail pieces was the result of
the 2006 renovation.

In addition to the two largest artifacts, the museum contains many different artifacts relating to the history of the city. Many famous people are represented through the display of their artifacts. Famous people who are represented include: Abraham Lincoln, George Washington, and Al Capone. Exhibits on the Great Chicago Fire, The Civil War, and Fort Dearborne are also present. One interesting artifact is the original letter "P" from the old Playboy headquarters.

Today the museum serves the community as both an educational resource and a community gathering place. In addition to the artifacts, the building houses a research center, galleries, museum store, and The History Café, a restaurant which is operated by celebrity Chef Wolfgang Puck. The museum keeps hours of 9:30 a.m. to 4:30 p.m., Monday through Saturday. On Sunday the museum is open from noon to 5:00 p.m.

Chicagoland Fun Fact

C. D. Peacock Jewelers was founded in 1837. It currently holds the distinction of being the oldest Chicago business still in existence today.

The Oriental Institute
1155 East 58th Street
Chicago, IL 60637
773-702-9514
www.oi.uchicago.edu
Free Admission Days: Always Free

Although the term Oriental usually conjures up images of all that is Chinese and Japanese, the Oriental Museum actually focuses on the countries of the "Near -East". Countries such as Egypt, Syria, Anatolia, and Mesopotamia make up much of the focus of the museum.

The museum is made up of a series of galleries, each pertaining to a specific geographical region. Each gallery contains ancient artifacts which enable visitors to learn what life was like in those ancient cultures. The artifacts contained in the museum have been gathered through the efforts of University of Chicago archeologists throughout the last 100 years. Pottery, tablets, and even remnants of clothing are all present at the museum.

The museum is home to more than just small artifacts though. Some very large items make their home at the museum. Some of these items include: statues, plaques, basins, and even masonry work. The museum is able to comfortably house some large pieces of work due to its expansive size. For those who are very interested in ancient artifacts, many hours can be spent perusing the collection.

The Oriental Museum is open Tuesday through Saturday from 10:00 a.m. until 6:00 p.m. On Sunday the museum keeps hours from noon until 6:00 p.m. It is advised that visitors check the web-site prior to their visit as the museum has a lengthy list of prohibited items.

Bartlett History Museum
228 South Main Street
Bartlett, IL 60103
630-837-0800
www.village.bartlett.il.us/museum/museumhistory.html
Free Admission Days: Always Free

In 1973, a group of local residents formed the Bartlett Historical Society partially because of the upcoming American Bicentennial of 1976. The young historical society saw the need to preserve the history of their community for the coming generations. With this goal the society set out to collect pieces of literature, photos, and historical items to illustrate the history of their town.

The early years of the Bartlett History Museum were modest to say the least. The museum consisted of a small exhibit inside the Bartlett Village Hall. Through much hard work the museum acquired a more fitting home in 1983, with the lease of a house on South Oak Street. The new location enabled the museum to grow and offer regular visiting hours. Just three years later the museum changed locations allowing for another expansion. The new location on 204 South Main provided a more convenient location and much more space.

In 1993, history repeated itself as the Bartlett History Museum once again moved into the Bartlett Village Hall. This time however, the museum would not be relegated to a couple of display cases. The Bartlett Village Hall had benefited from a large expansion, of which 1,200 square feet were dedicated for use by the museum. With this additional space the museum hired a professional curator, and introduced many community programs.

Currently the museum contains many interesting items from Bartlett's past. The museum is open Monday through Friday from 8:30 a.m. to 4:30 p.m. On Saturdays the museum keeps hours of 9:00 a.m. until noon.

Lombard Historical Museum

23 West Maple Street

Lombard, IL 60148

630-629-1885

www.reneau.us/lhm/lhm.html

Free Admission Days: Always Free

A project of the Lombard Historical Society, the Lombard Historical Museum provides visitors with a fine example of what life was like for residents of the community back in the late 1800's. The cottage style home was originally constructed for Chicago jewelry buyer Newell Matson. Matson decided to place the home in its present location due to its close proximity to the train station. Matson would commonly commute by train between Lombard and Chicago for business.

In 1972, the Lombard Historical Society reopened Mr. Matson's home as a museum dedicated to the lives of Lombard's citizens. The home was renovated and redecorated to represent the typical furnishings of the 1870's. The home is organized into four period rooms including a front parlor, back parlor, bedroom, and kitchen. The furnishings are all Victorian artifacts which were common during the post Civil War years. The most impressive room in the home is the front parlor. It was the front parlor which would be used to entertain guests during special occasions. Weddings, funerals, formal dinners, and holidays were all observed in the front parlor.

The Lombard Historical Museum is one of two historic homes owned by the Lombard Historical Society (the Sheldon Peck Homestead is the other and is listed on pg. 66). The Lombard Historical Museum is open on Wednesday and Sunday between the hours of 1:00 p.m. and 4:00 p.m. Additional hours are available by appointment. Please note that the Sheldon Peck Homestead and Lombard Historical Museum are never open on the same days, so visitors will need to spend two days in the area to see both.

West Chicago City Museum

132 Main Street

West Chicago, IL 60185

630-231-3376

www.westchicago.org/Museum/index.html

Free Admission Days: Always Free

The city of West Chicago was founded as the result of the development of the railroad industry in the area. Multiple rail lines from around the region happened to cross in this area resulting in the construction of some restaurants, hotels, and a fueling facility. Because of the development, the G&CU railroad constructed a mainline from the young township west to DeKalb and Fulton. The president of the railroad, John B. Turner, saw opportunity and organized the town and sold off lots. This selling of lots created an explosion of activity in the area. Dr. Joseph McConnell followed Turner's lead and also started subdividing their land. What resulted were two organized communities, Junction and Turner. Soon the towns would merge forming the town of Turner Junction.

Turner Junction would continue to grow as it provided a nice location to live, while allowing easy access to the luxuries of the big city of Chicago. Due to all of the rail lines, the town became a bedroom community for workers who would commute into Chicago for work and play. In order to attract more business, the town of Turner Junction changed its name to West Chicago in 1896. The name change worked as the town reincorporated as a city in 1906. Although the depression slowed its growth, the city would not be kept down for long. World War II provided business to several local industries, reenergizing the small city.

The City of West Chicago Museum is located in the 1884 former Turner Town Hall. The building, which was home to the police department, fire department, and government offices for over 90 years, is listed on the National Register of Historic Places. Since 1975, the city of West Chicago has sponsored the museum, whose purpose is to collect, preserve, and display the history of the city. The museum occupies two floors of the building and is home to many unique items and exhibits. Most of the artifacts from the museum were acquired directly from the residents of the city. Many of the artifacts pertain to the history of the local railroad industry and its effect on the growth of the area. In addition to the railroad artifacts, many artifacts which are present illustrate what life was like for residents of the area. Clothing, utensils, dishes, furniture, and quilts all give visitors a good feel for West Chicago life throughout the years. Artwork also has a special place at the museum. The museum contains works both owned by local residents and produced by local residents. Exhibits on the natural environment, government, and economy are also present.

The museum is open to the public Tuesday through Friday from 10:30 a.m. until 3:30 p.m. On Saturday the museum keeps hours of 11:00 a.m. until 3:00 p.m. Staff are available by phone Monday through Friday from 8:00 a.m. to 4:00 p.m. to answer questions about the museum as well as upcoming programs. For visitors free parking is available on the street as well as behind the museum.

Chicagoland Fun Fact

The Metropolitan Sanitary District of Greater Chicago is known as one of the seven engineering wonders of the United States.

HISTORICAL SITES

Jane Addams Hull-House Museum
University of Illinois @ Chicago
800 South Halstead
Chicago, IL 60607
312-413-5353
www.uic.edu/jaddams/hull
Free Admission Days: Always Free

In 1860, one of the great leaders in Chicago History was born. Jane Addams was one of the founders of the first settlement houses in the United States. The settlement house was an idea born in London, England as a possible answer to rising urban problems. The settlement houses were commonly located in poor neighborhoods, but were occupied by middle and upper class educated men and women. The settlement house movement increased so rapidly that soon over 100 houses were organized in the U.S. Chicago was a national leader of the phenomena as 35 settlement houses sprung up in the city by 1911.

The settlement houses were more than simply residences for the cultural elite. The houses served as community resource centers for their neighborhoods. Under the direction of Addams, the Hull-House provided many services to the working poor of the area. Job assistance, childcare, citizenship classes, and English instruction were all offered at the house. Surprisingly, the residents of the house even provided library services, as well as art and theatre classes. Because of the work going on at the various settlement houses, legislation against child labor and abuse became law.

So great was Jane Addams' influence on the world she was awarded the Nobel Peace Prize in 1931. Jane Addams died in 1935, but her memory lives on today at the Hull-House Museum. At the museum visitors can learn more about the Addams family and new social justice initiatives. Today the museum is open from 10:00 a.m. to 4:00 p.m., Tuesday through Friday. On Saturday the museum is open from noon to 4:00 p.m.

Batavia Depot Museum

155 Houston Street

Batavia, IL 60510

630-406-5274

Free Admission Days: Always Free

In 1911, the idea was born to create a historical society with the goal of preserving the history of the Batavia area. It wouldn't be until 1959 that that idea would take root and become a viable historical organization. John Gustafson, along with several others, was able to create an organization which would endure to this day. Under the leadership of Gustafson, the organization grew quickly from 45 founding members to 240 within the first year. Today the historical society remains strong at over 500 members.

The society is based out of the old Batavia Depot. The depot was constructed in 1854 and served the community for almost 100 years. After the demise of passenger rail service in the area the building remained vacant. In 1973, the building was uprooted and moved over nine blocks to its present location. After the move, and some refurbishing, the building was granted a coveted spot on the National Register of Historic Places in 1979. This designation came four years after the building's official dedication as the Batavia Depot Museum.

The museum stands today as a resource to all those who are interested in the history of the Batavia area. The museum contains artifacts and information pertaining to the town's beginning in 1833, when Christopher Payne became the area's first settler. The museum seeks to tell the story of Batavia's growth through industry, and its importance as a destination for Swedish immigrants who were displaced by the Great Chicago Fire of 1871.

Batavia's importance to the city of Chicago is also illustrated through displays which tell the story of the Batavia quarries which produced a great portion of the limestone used during the reconstruction of Chicago.

Many more stories are told including that of Bellevue Place. Bellevue Place, a women's sanitarium started by Dr. R. J. Patterson in 1867, served many women including the widow Mary Todd Lincoln. Special attention is given to the windmill industry which dominated the area for many decades. There are actually many windmills which have been reconstructed and placed along the river walk as a tribute to this important industry. The manufacturing of windmills was so prevalent in Batavia that the town acquired the title of "Windmill Capital of the World" during the late 1800's.

Today visitors can spend much time exploring the museum, caboose, and the river walk. The museum boasts a volunteer staff of over 100 people who staff the museum, lead tours, catalogue artifacts, and raise much needed funds. The museum's volunteers also help with the research efforts of the Gustafson Research Center. The Gustafson Research Center serves a resource to those who want to study the in-depth history of Batavia. The center also serves as a valuable resource to those who wish to trace the lineage of former Batavia residents.

Currently the museum keeps hours of 2:00 p.m. to 4:00 p.m. on Monday, Wednesday, Friday, Saturday, and Sunday. The museum is open seasonally from the time between March and Thanksgiving. It is strongly advised that visitors call ahead to verify the museum will be open on the day they intend to visit.

Glessner House Museum

1800 South Prairie Avenue

Chicago, IL 60616

312-326-1480

www.glessnerhouse.org

Free Admission Days: Wednesday

In 1887, a home was built which would have a dramatic impact on the
field of architecture. The Glessner House was designed by architect
Henry Hobson Richardson. The home would be the last designed by
Richardson as he actually died a year before it was completed. The home
was not the traditional Victorian architectural design of the day. The
home's biggest effect was not on the Glessners, who lived there, but
rather a young person by the name of Frank Lloyd Wright. Wright
would become one of the most famous architects in history, and the
Glessner House served as one of his first inspirations.

The home, which is listed on the National Register of Historic Places, is
known for its imposing exterior. The home's design was so radical that
the neighbors often complained about the aesthetics of the building. The
inside of the home however, could not be more inviting. Oak paneling,
beautiful art, highly crafted furniture, and a courtyard bring about a sense
of warmth.

Inside the home resides the actual museum. Over 6000 pieces tell the
history of the home, as well as of its occupants. Vases, glass, and
furniture can all be seen. Picture frames and wood carvings allow visitors
to get a feel for how wealthy the Glessner family was.

At the Glessner House Museum visitors get to experience a high level of
service. Visitors are guided around the home by highly experienced and
intelligent docents. Tours last about an hour and visitors will learn more
about the home and the high society life of Chicago in the late 1800's.
Visitors are advised to call ahead for hours of operation.

Historic Pleasant Home

217 Home Avenue

Oak Park, IL 60302

708-383-2654

www.oprf.com/phf/

Free Admission Days: Always Free

In 1897, architect George W. Maher began to design a 30 room mansion which would become a prime example of the Prairie School architecture movement. The home, which stands in at 16,000 square feet, makes use of a variety of natural materials and motifs. The motifs used are an example of the "motif-rhythm" theory which was made famous by Maher.

From the outside the house has a very strong appearance. While light on ornamentation, the house exudes an image of strength, durability, and class. Rectangular windows, full length porch, and sturdy square columns reinforce a feeling of stability. While the outside may be rather plain, the inside is dazzling.

The interior of the home is decorated with plentiful amounts of art glass, woodwork, and fancy rugs. A large fireplace dominates the foyer providing both a focal point and warmth. Bookcases with lion's heads carved into them dominate the library area. Lion's heads are prevalent throughout the house as one of the motifs. Mosaic floors decorate the breakfast nook, as well as the dining porch.

The very ornamented home is the only George W. Maher designed home that is currently open to the public. The hours of the home vary and can be discovered by calling ahead.

Joliet Iron Works Historic Site

Columbia Street

Joliet, IL 60433

815-727-8700

www.fpdwc.org/ironworks.cfm

Free Admission Days: Always Free

The reason that Joliet is referred to as the "City of Steel" is because of the influence of the Joliet Iron Works facility. Located a stones throw from the imposing 1858 Joliet Penitentiary, the remains of the Iron Works facility can still be seen today. The Iron Works opened in 1869, and became one of the dominant employers of the area. During its peak production period the facility employed around 2,000 workers. For just over 60 years the facility used the abundant local limestone to produce their product. The steel produced in Joliet was used primarily for barbed wire and railroad ties. From Joliet steel were crafted many of the tools needed to farm the growing mid-west region.

When the Iron Works closed up shop it was dismantled. The site remained unused for 60 years until the Forest Preserve District of Will County purchased the land in 1990. Due to some forward thinking on the District's part, the old facility was converted into an outdoor museum. Today the ruins of the facility remain, but there are now paths which guide visitors around the grounds. There are also many informational kiosks which tell the history behind each area of the park. Interestingly, some of the kiosks contain photos of what the facility looked like in its heyday.

Tours of the facility are mildly rigorous (some steps), and largely self guided. Interestingly, each Sunday morning at 9:00 a.m. there is a free volunteer led tour of the facility. The hours for the site are 8:00 a.m. to 8:00 p.m. during the summer, and 8:00 a.m. to 5:00 p.m. during the winter.

William L. Gregg House Museum
117 South Linden Avenue
Westmont, IL 60559
630-963-5259
http://www.wpd4fun.org/index_2.htm
Free Admission Days: Always Free

For over 125 years the William L. Gregg House has served as a local landmark in the Westmont community. The home was built as a showpiece for the Excelsior Brick Company which was one of may brick producing companies in the area. The 1872 home was owned by William L. Gregg who started his company that same year. Gregg would later become the most prominent brick company owner in the area.

Always a forward thinker, Gregg came up with many innovations for his company. Firstly Gregg located his company on a high piece of land. This enabled the shipments of completed bricks to be delivered downhill. Mr. Gregg also developed the triple pressure brick machine. The new machine enabled Gregg to manufacture bricks which could withstand over 100,000 pounds of pressure. At its peak the company employed 120 people and produced upwards of 70,000 bricks daily. Unfortunately for the community its entire brick industry essentially died out by 1900.

The legacy of Westmont's brick making industry remains today in the form of Gregg's House. The home, which is listed on the Register of Historic Places, has housed a museum since 1981. In addition to its museum mission, the home is the location for many programs of a historical nature throughout the year. At the rear of the home is a splendid outdoor garden. The home is open on Wednesdays and Sundays from 1:00 p.m. until 3:00 p.m.

Sheldon Peck Homestead

355 East Parkside Avenue

Lombard, IL 60148

630-629-1885

www.reneau.us/apeck6/peck0.html

Free Admission Days: Always Free

In addition to the Lombard Historical Museum, the Lombard Historical Society operates the Sheldon Peck Homestead. The Sheldon Peck Homestead is the oldest home in Lombard. The home was constructed by portrait artist Sheldon Peck in 1939. Peck moved to the area from Chicago after a downturn in the portrait business left his family in a state of financial difficulty. After selling his Chicago property Peck and his family relocated to the Lombard area and began their new lives as farmers.

In addition to their lives as farmers the Peck family was an integral part of the Underground Railroad. The Peck homestead became known as the center point for the anti-slavery movement of the area. As a staunch abolitionist Peck represented the views of many of the area's citizens. As a "Station Master" of the Underground Railroad Peck put himself in legal jeopardy from 1850, until the time the 13th Amendment was ratified.

Today the story of the Peck family is told at the homestead. The homestead, which opened to the public in 1999, has been renovated to resemble how it would have looked during the 1840's. Period items and furniture are present in the home giving the visitor a true feel for 1840's life. Outside the home is a garden which contains specimens of the very plants which the Peck's would have raised, thus rounding out the historical experience.

The Sheldon Peck Homestead is open from 1:00 p.m. to 4:00 p.m. on Tuesdays and Saturdays.

The Farmhouse Museum

399 Buesterfield Road

Elk Grove Village, IL 60007

847-439-3994

Free Admission Days: Always Free

Established in 1976, the Farmhouse Museum is part of a museum campus which serves to teach visitors about pioneer life in the mid-west. The farmhouse was built in the 1850's and served as the home place for the Schuette clan. The farmhouse is filled with many period furnishings as well as utensils and tools. The museum specializes in displaying artifacts from the period between 1860 and 1900. In addition to artifacts about farming, the story of the founding of Elk Grove, and its history, is also told at the farmhouse.

The farmhouse is not the only building which sets on the museum campus. The campus includes a schoolhouse which serves as an orientation center for the facility. A late 1800's era barn also sets on the museum campus. The barn contains many fine examples of farm machinery and tools of the 19th century. A chicken coop and privy also grace the grounds of the campus. Since no farm is complete without vegetables, the museum campus contains a vegetable and herb garden which is actively cultivated during the warm summer months.

The Farmhouse Museum, and museum campus, are open on Wednesdays from 2:30 p.m. to 5:30 p.m., Fridays from 9:00 a.m. to noon, and Saturdays from 11:00 a.m. to 2:00 p.m.

Lisle Station Museum
921 School Street
Lisle, IL 60532
630-968-0499
http://www.lisleparkdistrict.org/museum.htm
Free Admission Days: Always Free

For over 30 years the Lisle Station Museum has been a place for the preservation of history. The museum was the result of the cooperation of the Lisle Park District, Lisle Heritage Society, and the Village Government. The three organizations saw the opportunity to create a museum, at the same time allowing for the preservation of the historic train depot.

For over 100 years the depot served the community as its transportation hub, and lifeline to the world beyond. The busy depot shipped passengers and freight allowing Lisle to prosper during the 19th century. The history of those exiting days is persevered at the museum today. Currently the Lisle Station Museum consists of six buildings on its museum campus. The heart of the museum is the depot building itself. The building today holds a variety of artifacts from Lisle's rail-road days. The building also tells the story of Lisle, from its founding in 1932, to the present day. Special areas of the depot building include the living quarters, waiting room, and ticket office. Outside of the depot are several other buildings. The Netzley-Yender farmhouse, Beaubien Tavern, 1882 Caboose, and Blacksmith's Shop all give visitors a first hand look at life in 19th century Northern Illinois.

The Lisle Station Museum is a seasonal attraction open between April and December. Normal hours for the museum are 1:00 p.m. until 4:00 p.m., Tuesday, Saturday, and Sunday. Tours for groups are available at other times by appointment.

RELIGIOUS SITES

Conventual Franciscan Friars of Marytown

1600 West Park Avenue

Libertyville, IL 60048

847-367-7800

www.marytown.com

Free Admission Days: Always Free

Since 1928, Marytown has served as a home for devout persons who have given their lives in service to God. The idea for Marytown came about in 1925 when the Benedictine sisters of Clyde, Missouri requested permission from Cardinal Mundelein to open a new convent. Three years later the convent was opened and 33 of the Clyde convent's sisters were sent to occupy the new location. From 1928 until 1978 the Benedictine sisters resided at the convent, producing sacramental bread, as well as producing most of the goods required for their own survival.

In 1978, the sisters re-located back to Missouri, turning over Marytown to the Conventual Franciscan Friars. The friars have kept up the tradition of prayer, maintaining the practice of perpetual adoration. Perpetual adoration is the practice of praying 24 hours per day, every day. The practice of perpetual adoration originated in France during the 13th century. The perpetual adoration program at Marytown has been in effect since June 7, 1928. Special effort is taken to ensure that the chapel is open 24 hours per day, with friars and lay-people constantly offering prayers to God.

Making the duties of perpetual adoration easier is the sheer beauty of the chapel. The chapel is decorated with jewels, marble, gold leaf, and gold plating. Mosaics and stained glass play an important role in adding color to the chapel. The chapel contains 11 stained glass windows, each depicting images from the Bible. Over 20 mosaics depict images such as the Eucharist, the Joys and Glories of the Virgin Mary, and Christ the King. Some of the most striking features of the chapel are the 38 marble columns which run along the length of the chapel. The columns, each one dedicated to a Catholic saint, are crafted from six different types of marble.

Outside of the shrine are 14 acres of land dedicated to fostering feelings of peace and tranquility. Gardens, statues, flowers, and paths all allow visitors to engage in quiet reflection and communion with nature. Some of the more popular outdoor constructions are the Stations of the Cross, the St. Maximilian Kolbe Rose Garden, and the St. Francis of Assisi Peace Garden. The outdoors can be appreciated year round, but is especially inviting during spring and early summer.

In 1999, a new addition was made to Marytown with the addition of the Kolbe/Holocaust Exhibit. The exhibit tells the story of Maximilian Kolbe's time in Auschwitz. The Nazis imprisoned Kolbe for his role as a teacher of religious thought. Since Kolbe had quite a following, the Nazis felt threatened by his ability to influence the thoughts of the general public through his writings and periodicals. While at Auschwitz, Kolbe served his fellow prisoners as a spiritual leader, organizing and celebrating mass in secret. Kolbe's defining moment came in 1941 when he gave his life to save that of another prisoner. Because of his influence and unselfishness Kolbe was conferred the honor of sainthood by Pope John Paul II in 1982.

Marytown is open year round, with the chapel being open 24 hours per day. Information about the Kolbe Exhibit, retreat programs, and the bookstore can be accessed through Marytown's website or by calling ahead.

Baha'i House of Worship of North America

100 Linden Avenue

Wilmette, IL 60091

847-853-2300

www.bahai.us/bahai-temple

Free Admission Days: Always Free

In 1908, the first parcel of land was purchased on which the first temple of the Baha'i Faith in America would be built. The Baha'i Faith was founded in 1844 by Baha'u'llah, the son of a Persian nobleman. Born as a Muslim, Baha'u'llah envisioned his faith as one that combined the basic tenants which all of the world's major religions shared. What resulted from Baha'u'llah's vision was a faith that he described to be a reflection of all of the major religions. Over time the religion that Baha'u'llah founded spread across the globe. Today there are over 5,000,000 Baha'i Faith practitioners located in over 260 countries. The Baha'i Faith is actually only second to Christianity in the number of countries in which it is practiced.

The center of the Baha'i Faith in America is located at the temple in Wilmette. The temple cornerstone was dedicated in 1912, but due to war and depression the temple's construction would take decades to complete. The design of the temple was the creation of French Canadian architect Louis Bourgeois. Bourgeois' design immediately gained worldwide attention as being innovative as well as artistic. The temple design features extensive use of concrete, making the temple stand out with its bright white exterior. Even though it is a concrete structure, the outside was designed to mimic the pattern of lace. Placed within the lacy design are symbols of the world's major religions. The symbols of world religions pay respect to the values on which the Baha'i Faith was built.

Inside the temple the lacy appearance continues. The domed ceiling allows light to pass through symbolizing the unity between religions which the Baha'i Faith seeks to promote. The dome stretches 135 feet from the top to the floor. The visitor's center is located inside the temple. The visitor's center has an abundant amount of information for those interested in the building of the temple, as well as information about the Baha'i Faith.

Probably the most popular aspect of the Baha'i House of Worship of North America are the gardens located outside the temple building. Baha'i temples are well known for the quality and beauty of their surrounding gardens. The grounds at Wilmette are home to fountains, trees, shrubs, and dozens of varieties of flowers. The most notable of the flowers are the 20,000 tulips that are planted each year.

Yearly over 250,000 visitors come and see the temple and its surrounding gardens. The temple itself is open from 7:00 a.m. to 10:00 p.m. daily. The visitor's center keeps varied hours, mostly ranging from 10:00 a.m. to 8:00 p.m. in the warmer months to 10:00 a.m. to 5:00 p.m. during the cooler months

Chicagoland Fun Fact

Wilmette is regarded as a bedroom community in the affluent North Shore district.

Rockefeller Memorial Chapel

5850 South Woodlawn Avenue

Chicago, IL 60637

773-702-2100

http://rockefeller.uchicago.edu

Free Admission Days: Always Free

Between 1925 and 1928, construction of the chapel for the University of Chicago took place. The Rockefeller Memorial Chapel was made possible by a grant from John D. Rockefeller. Throughout the years Rockefeller donated upwards of $35 million to the university, earmarking $1.5 million for the construction of the chapel. Although construction did not begin until 1925, the chapel was actually designed in 1918 by renowned architect Bertram Goodhue. Goodhue was known as an innovator, as well as a master of the Gothic style. Goodhue's design incorporated Gothic elements into a Byzantine/Romanesque style. This combination of styles enables the chapel to stand apart from the rest of the buildings at the university.

The design of Goodhue is an engineering marvel, as well as an architectural beauty. The chapel is unique for the fact that it is constructed from stone and concrete without the use of steel. This lack of steel required Goodhue to make the most efficient use of his materials. Because of the weight of the structure (said to be over 32,000 tons) the foundations of the building extend 80 feet into the ground. Due to the look of the structure, much effort was taken by Goodhue to complement its imposing appearance.

One unique feature of the chapel is its pastel stained glass windows. The stained glass windows are unique in their use of understated colors. Goodhue chose pastel colors so that the light they created would not draw attention away from the inner ornamentation of the building. As far as the inner ornamentation of the building goes, sculptures dominate. Approximately 80 sculptures are present in the chapel. The sculptures depict a variety of people ranging from Plato, Moses, Jesus Christ,

St. Francis, Zoroaster, and Isaiah. Interestingly there is actually a statue of Goodhue himself, which was placed in the chapel after his death.

In addition to the statues, mosaics, colorful medallions, and wood carvings adorn the cathedral. The organ is worthy of special regard due to its carvings by Alois Lang. The carvings, which also decorate the south balcony, were carved from white Appalachian oak.

Even with all of its design features and ornamentation, the most noticeable thing about the chapel is its sheer size. The chapel measures 265 feet long and over 100 feet wide. The north side chapel tower measures 207 feet tall and contains 277 steps. The Laura Spelman Rockefeller Memorial Carillon is the second largest carillon in the world (based on mass). The carillon contains 72 bells which reportedly also makes it the world's second largest musical instrument. Because of its size, the 1700 seat chapel plays host to church services, weddings, lectures, concerts, and film screenings.

The Rockefeller Memorial Chapel is open daily from 8:00 a.m. until 4:00 p.m. Tours of the carillon are available to the public at 11:30 a.m. and 5:30 p.m., Monday through Friday. On Sunday tours are also given immediately following worship services. Meeting places for the tours are outside the tower entrance for weekday tours, and by the pulpit for Sunday tours.

The National Shrine of St. Therese

8501 Bailey Road

Darien, IL 60561

630-969-4141

www.saint-therese.org

Free Admission Days: Always Free

In Darien is located the largest collection of artifacts, outside of France, pertaining to St. Therese of Lisieux. St. Therese was born in 1873, the last of nine children. Due to her being the baby of the family, and the death of her mother when Therese was only four years old, young Therese became a very spoiled little girl. Her father and siblings rained affection down on her, leading her to become a very self-absorbed youth.

In 1886, young Therese had a conversion of spirit which changed her behavior and her life's direction. Because of this conversion, the self-absorbed child gave way to a responsible and charitable young woman. At age 15, Therese joined the Carmelite convent in Lisieux and began to dedicate her life to God. At the convent Therese lived the normal life of a nun, but she did impress her peers with her deep devotion and personal relationship with God.

In 1897, at only age 24, Therese died from tuberculosis. Therese was able to make a lasting impression on the Catholic Church and the world through her autobiography, *Story of a Soul*. Due to the influence of her writing, the church bestowed the title of Sainthood on her in 1925. Today the National Shrine of St. Therese serves as America's monument to this important Catholic saint. The Shrine is open daily from 10:00 a.m. to 4:00 p.m. In addition to the beautiful shrine there is also a gift shop stocked with many religious items.

Billy Graham Center Museum

Wheaton College

500 College Avenue

Wheaton, IL 60187

630-752-5909

http://bgc.gospelcom.net

Free Admission Days: Always Free

Wheaton College is home to a museum which contains a large collection of artifacts pertaining to the most famous minister in American history, Billy Graham. While the museum is not officially a "Billy Graham Museum" it does serve to detail the history behind his life and ministry. The museum was designed to pay homage to Rev. Graham's rural upbringing and his worldwide ministry. The museum itself takes the shape of a typical mid-west dairy barn. Instead of typical barn doors, visitors actually enter the museum at the base of a large cross which has been cut out of the side of the building.

Once inside, the rural feeling continues as visitors are greeted by an animatronic cow named Bessie. Bessie is a representation of an actual cow that young Billy Graham would milk every morning. Bessie tells visitors stories about Rev. Graham's youth, his work on the farm, and even sings songs. Bessie also challenges kids to search for specific items within the museum. Surprisingly there are a small, but vocal, number of folks who do not approve of Bessie, stating Bessie is not appropriate to honor Rev. Graham. At the insistence of the Graham family, Bessie will stay at the museum in an effort to engage the interest of the museum's younger visitors.

After visiting with Bessie visitors have the opportunity to check out the temporary exhibit space. Periodically the museum displays different works which pertain to Jesus Christ and Christian ministry. The museum's permanent exhibits begin with a series of tapestries, each depicting great Christian leaders throughout the centuries. St. Francis,

Martin Luther, and Blaise Paschal, among others, are featured in the full color tapestries.

Continuing through the museum visitors have the opportunity to learn more about the growth of Christianity and evangelization in America. Various artifacts including a portion of the first Bible printed in the U.S., Civil War Scripture books, circuit rider saddle bags, and 18th century sermons are included in the collection. The collection spans the time period from 1492 until the end of World War II. In addition to the artifacts, information on the time period is presented through the use of dioramas, audio clips, and other interactive media.

The museum tour continues with a stop in front of the *Cross of the Millennium*. The Frederick Hart creation is located in a dark circular room and consists of a translucent cross with surrounding glass etched with bible verses. Light is cast through the verses and cross providing a brilliant effect for the viewer.

The main attraction of the museum is the *The Life and Ministry of Billy Graham* exhibit. The exhibit details the life of Rev. Graham from his time spent as a youth on a farm, to his life as a world wide religious figure. Videos from Rev. Graham's crusades, interviews, and news stories can all be viewed at the museum. Gifts from various heads of states and celebrities are also on display. The traveling pulpit, complete with sermon notes, is also displayed.

The final exhibit in the museum is the *Walk Through the Gospel* exhibit. *The Walk Through the Gospel* exhibit is a 3-D recreation of Jan Styka's Glendale, California masterpiece. The exhibit leads from the Styka painting to a room featuring the resurrection. The Billy Graham Center Museum also has a gift shop and a prayer chapel. The museum is open from 9:30 a.m. to 5:30 p.m., Monday through Saturday. On Sundays the museum is open from 1:00 p.m. to 5:00 p.m.

ART GALLERIES AND MUSEUMS

The Art Institute of Chicago

111 South Michigan Avenue

Chicago, IL 60603

312-443-3600

www.artic.edu/aic

Free Admission Days: Varies by Season

Since 1897, the Art Institute of Chicago has served as both a museum
and a school dedicated to training and featuring its artist students. Since
1893, the museum has been located at its present location. The
institute's building was designed in the Beaux-Arts style by the firm of
Shepley, Rutan, and Coolidge. Over the years, the spacious building has
allowed the school to grow and develop the talents of many fine artists.
Many famous painters, sculptors, and filmmakers have been educated at
the institute. Artists spending time at the institute include: Walt Disney,
Orson Wells, Georgia O'Keefe, and even Hugh Heffner!

The institute's classes are unique in the fact that there are no grades
assigned. All classes are marked as pass or fail. Due to the subjective
nature of art, the institute has found that this grading system serves to
eliminate bias on the part of the professor. The unique grading system
has also allowed students to push the envelope of artistic expression.
Over its history, the institute has proudly displayed controversial pieces
of art as part of its mission. Due to the institute's willingness to push the
envelope, it has periodically suffered funding cuts from business and
government. Overall, artistic expression does eventually win out making
the museum a leader in cutting edge art.

All of the art at the institute is not controversial though. The collection
of the institute contains many fine French paintings, American
masterpieces, Asian art, as well as sculptures, drawings, prints, and
photographs. Over 5,000 years of art history are on display at the
institute.

Today the institute's museum is open from 10:30 a.m. to 5:00 p.m., Monday, Tuesday, Wednesday, and Friday. On Thursday the museum is open from 10:30 a.m. to 8:00 p.m. On weekends the museum keeps hours from 10:00 a.m. until 5:00 p.m. Do be sure to call ahead, or visit the web site, as the museum offers free admission at various times throughout the year.

Chicagoland Fun Fact

During 1884 a cholera epidemic swept Chicago, killing over 5% of the city's population.

Skokie Northshore Sculpture Park

McCormick Boulevard

Skokie, IL 60076

847-679-4265

www.sculpturepark.org

Free Admission Days: Always Free

Located in Skokie is one of the most unique fusions of the arts and nature in Illinois. The Skokie Northshore Sculpture Park was the result of two separate groups who both wanted the land the park currently occupies to be put to good use. The community government wanted to create a recreational park with playgrounds, trails, and picnic areas. A group of private citizens longed for a sculpture park focusing on contemporary works of art. What resulted from both groups' interests is a park complete with benches, jogging trails, bike paths, and 72 sculptures.

The sculptures at the park range in size from the very small to the very large. Materials used to construct the sculptures include: wood, metal, stone, and wire. The park is home to various community and artistic events. The park's web-site has free downloadable self-guided tour information, as well as a family oriented activity guide. The web site also lists each sculpture's name, artist, and what it is made from.

The two mile long park is open year round for all to enjoy.

Mary and Leigh Block Museum of Art

40 Arts Circle Drive

Evanston, IL 60208

847-491-4000

www.blockmuseum.northwestern.edu

Free Admission Days: Always Free

The Mary and Leigh Block Museum of Art was founded as a result of funds which were donated, to Northwestern University, for the purpose of building and housing a collection of university owned art. The generosity of the Blocks allowed the university to eventually construct a new building to house the university's growing collection. Before there was a permanent exhibit space, the university's art was scattered around campus. Due to the art being spread out it was not easy for visitors to see, nor was it easy for students to use for study and inspiration.

In 2000, the pieces of art were gathered up and placed in the new building. The building was designed by Chicago architect Dirk Lohan. Lohan's design called for the generous use of limestone and glass. The new building enables the gallery to maintain a collection of over 4,000 pieces.

The pieces of art at the gallery consist mainly of works on paper. Prints and photographs dominate the collection. One interesting art form on display is computer-mediated art. This new type of artwork makes use of computers and software programs to craft artistic images which serve to inspire as well as entertain.

In addition to the regular collection, the museum features ongoing temporary exhibitions. It is possible to visit the museum often and see different works each time. One collection the museum is noted for is the Theo Leffmann collection. Leffman's works reside in their own gallery and consist of textile pieces.

In addition to printed art, the museum also hosts film screenings, lectures, and classes in its 160 seat Pick-Laudati Auditorium. The museum keeps hours of 10:00 a.m. to 8:00 p.m., Wednesday through Friday, and 10:00 a.m. to 5:00 p.m., Tuesday, Saturday, and Sunday. The museum is closed on Mondays. Parking around the museum is free after 4:00 p.m. weekdays, and is free all day on weekends. Parking during other hours is $6.00, and parking passes can be purchased at the University Parking Office on Hinman Avenue.

Chicagoland Fun Fact:

Evanston is a common filming location for major motion pictures. Films including: *Uncle Buck, Dennis The Menace, Home Alone, Home Alone 2, Home Alone 3, Sixteen Candles, Road to Perdition, Rookie of the Year*, and *The Princess Bride* were at least partially filmed in Evanston.

Intuit: The Center for Intuitive and Outsider Art

756 North Milwaukee Avenue

Chicago, IL 60622

312-243-9088

www.art.org

Free Admission Days: Always Free

Since 1991, Chicago has been a focal point in an art movement known as outsider-or intuitive-art. Outsider and intuitive art works are those which have been produced by artists with either limited formal training, or limited outside influence from established artists. Much of the work which falls into the category of outsider art is also referred to as folk art, visionary art, and self-taught art. One aspect of outsider art is the variety of materials which are used. Everything from bottle caps to hay can be utilized. Quilts, tinwork, mobiles, and drawings are common as outsider art pieces.

The center's building is organized into two gallery spaces and a performance area. The gallery in the front hosts temporary exhibits, while the back Study Gallery is home to the organization's permanent collection. Throughout the year the organization hosts a variety of lectures pertaining to the field of outsider art. The galleries, which take about one hour to enjoy, are open Tuesday through Saturday from 11:00 a.m. to 5:00 p.m. On Thursdays the facility stays open a bit later, closing down at 7:30 p.m.

National Museum of Mexican Art

1852 West 19th Street

Chicago, IL 60608

312-738-1503

www.nationalmuseumofmexicanart.org

Free Admission Days: Always Free

Located in the Pilson/Little Village Communities, the National Museum of Mexican Art serves the Chicagoland area as its center of Latino culture and history. The museum also has the distinction of being the only museum of Latino culture to be accredited by the American Association of Museums. Boasting a collection of over 5,000 objects, the museum also has one of the largest collections of Mexican art in the United States.

The museum got its start in 1982 due in large part to the efforts of Carlos Tortolero. In 1987, the museum moved into its current location in Harrison Park. 2001 brought about the most radical change in the museum's history as it tripled in size. The expansion was necessary due to the addition of modern storage vaults and galleries.

Today the museum maintains its mission of sharing the Mexican culture and heritage will all those who are interested. The museum's main exhibit *Mexicanidad: Our Past is Present* tells the story of Mexico, from prehistory to the present day. Special attention is also paid to the experiences of Mexican people in the United States . In addition to the main exhibit, visitors will be treated to a variety of colorful paintings, weavings, and painted pottery. October is a great time to visit due to the annual *Dia de los Muertos* ("Day of the Dead") exhibit.

The museum is open from 10:00 a.m. until 5:00 p.m., Tuesday through Sunday.

Elmhurst Art Museum

150 Cottage Hill Avenue

Elmhurst, IL 60126

630-834-0202

www.elmhurstartmuseum.org

Free Admission Days: Tuesdays Free

In 1974, a group of Elmhurst citizens organized with the goal of building an art center. By 1983, the group had formed a museum which occupied two rooms in the Elmhurst Community Center. In 1990, plans were made to purchase a larger and more permanent home for the museum. The old McCormick house was purchased by the group and was moved to its present site in 1994. The home was used as the cornerstone of the museum, and the museum was in turn built around the house.

What made the house owned by Robert H. McCormick unique was its use of glass, brick, and steel in its construction. The house itself was to serve as a prototype for future row houses, and was designed by renowned architect Mies van der Rohe. Mies van der Rohe made his name through his design efforts of Chicago's great steel and glass towers. The home was designed to serve as a representation of a single story of one of the towers of Lake Shore Drive. Although the architect had a penchant for the finer things, the home he designed was made to be built inexpensively. Concrete floors, basic glass, cork, and pre-fabricated panels were all used in the home. Today the museum considers the home as the most important piece in the museum's collection.

The museum's collection and scope has grown over the years. For the first 16 years the museum exclusively displayed works from mid-western artists. Today the museum displays works from around the world. Various exhibitions and events are held throughout the year at the museum, as the museum also acts as the cultural center of the community. The museum opens at various times but usually closes at 4:00 p.m., be sure to call ahead for exact times.

DePaul University Museum
2350 North Kenmore Avenue
Chicago, IL 60614
773-325-7506
http://museums.depaul.edu/artwebsite
Free Admission Days: Always Free

From its founding in 1898, to the 1970's, the DePaul University art collection lacked organization. Most works during that time were acquired through donation and displayed wherever it was convenient. In the 1970's the Women's Board spearheaded an effort to set a direction to the university's art collecting efforts. What resulted from their efforts was the DePaul University Museum.

Today the museum serves the university, and community, as a showcase of art from all over the world. Paintings from the famous masters, photographs, and sculptures can all be seen at the museum. As part of the university's mission, the museum displays an impressive collection of mid-western art. Most of the mid-western art dates from the mid 1900's and a lot of it focuses on mid-western life.

In addition to the masters and the mid-western art, many temporary exhibits take place throughout the year. Many of the traveling exhibits focus on the art of a particular culture. In the past Iraqi, German, and Dutch art have been displayed. Exhibits change often so be sure to check out the museum's web-site to see what will be there.

The museum is open seven days per week. Monday through Thursday the hours are 11:00 a.m. to 5:00 p.m. On Friday the museum stays open until 7:00 p.m. On weekends the museum keeps hours of noon to 5:00 p.m.

The Renaissance Society

5811 South Ellis Avenue

Bergman Gallery, Cobb Hall 418

Chicago, IL 60637

773-702-8670

www.renaissancesociety.org

Free Admission Days: Always Free

Located at the University of Chicago, The Renaissance Society seeks to share the world of contemporary art with its visitors. Through this sharing, the society seeks to encourage the growth of the field as well as people understanding of the art. Since 1915, the society has shared the world of contemporary art through events, publications, and its own exhibitions.

Throughout the years the society has hosted exhibitions from cutting edge artists like Picasso, Mondrian, Marc Chagall, and Gertrude Stein. One of the most famous exhibitions hosted by the society was the Alexander Calder mobile exhibition of 1934. This exhibition was the first American appearance of this legendary artist.

Today many artists make their American and mid-west debuts at the society. Exhibitions change about every six weeks and cover a wide variety of artistic mediums. Some of the exhibits are colorful, some try to make the viewer think, and others are simply head scratchers. The society museum is open from 10:00 a.m. to 5:00 p.m., Tuesday through Friday. On weekends the museum is open from noon to 5:00 p.m.

The Museum of Contemporary Art

220 East Chicago Avenue

Chicago, IL 60611

312-280-2660

www.mcachicago.org

Free Admission Days: Tuesdays Free

The story of the Museum of Contemporary Art began on East Ontario Street in a building which had formerly housed the corporate offices of Playboy Enterprises. The first years of the museum were eventful, beginning with the 1969 wrapping of the building in 8,000 square feet of tarpaulin by famed artist Christo, to the performance of Chris Burdin who laid under a sheet of glass for 45 hours. For almost 30 years the museum hosted many wild events and exhibitions which were avant garde in nature.

1996 proved to be a milestone year in the history of the museum. Due to the museum's popularity, during its first 30 years, much more space was needed. The museum had tried a system of buying up the properties around the original building, renovating them and filling them up with their artwork. Eventually, that became unmanageable and the present building was constructed. Complete with a sculpture garden, the present building contains over 45,000 square feet dedicated to exhibit space. This exhibit space represents seven times more square feet than the original building. The current building was designed by German Architect Josef Paul Kleihues. The building makes use of limestone and aluminum, and was the fist American building to be designed by Kleihues. The opening of the new building was so anticipated by the community that over 25,000 people came to visit the new building during a special 24 hour public preview period.

The museum, which only features art produced since 1945, also contains an art library, education center, 300 seat theatre, museum store, and a restaurant which is overseen by celebrity chef Wolfgang Puck. The museum itself possesses 5,600 objects in its permanent collection. The real bread and butter of the museum are the traveling exhibitions. Influential artists such as Andy Warhol, Jasper Johns, and Antoni Tapie have all been displayed at the museum. Local artists have also been given their time to shine at the museum. Dan Peterman, Jo Anne Carlson, and Paul Rosin (among others) have also been given their chance to shine at the museum.

Today the museum is open from 10:00 a.m. to 8:00 p.m. on Tuesdays. Wednesday through Sunday the museum keeps hours of 10:00 a.m. to 5:00 p.m. The museum is closed every Monday, and also on Thanksgiving, Christmas, and New Year's Day. Although the museum is a largely self guided affair, the museum does offer guided tours on certain days, be sure to call ahead for more information.

Chicagoland Fun Fact

On April 21, 1855 the Lager Beer Riot, a protest against the Sunday closing of taverns and saloons, occurred thus becoming Chicago's first major civil disturbance.

Antioch Fine Arts Foundation Gallery

983 Main Street

Antioch, IL 60002

847-838-2274

www.antiochfinearts.org

Located two blocks north of Route 173 is the center of the arts scene of Antioch, Illinois. The Antioch Fine Arts Foundation Gallery serves the local arts scene as a resource for members to connect with local residents and arts connoisseurs. The gallery consists of three rooms which serve to display works from separate artists on a monthly basis.

The White Room, Sage Room, and the Terra Cotta Room, are re-hung every month with new works from the foundations' member artists. The mediums on display change every month and range from photography, to painting, to sculpture, to crafts. The works on display are usually offered for sale and range in price from $30 to over $3,000.

Fortunately for visitors, most of the fun to be had at the gallery is free of charge. In addition to viewing the spectacular art, free music events are common. The gallery commonly hosts folk music and classical music groups. The folk music group is a very active group and performs every month. The classical group performs less frequently so you will need to check with the museum for dates. The gallery is commonly open from 10:00 a.m. to 4:00 p.m., Thursday through Saturday. On Sundays the gallery keeps hours of noon to 4:00 p.m.

Union Street Gallery

1527 Otto Boulevard

Chicago Heights, IL 60411

708-754-2601

www.unionstreetgallery.org

Free Admission Days: Always Free

For over ten years the Union Street Gallery has served the Chicago Heights area as an art development center and exhibition space. The gallery itself contains works from both emerging and established artists. The gallery takes advantage of the membership of the Collaborative Arts Guild in order to present many interesting and eclectic pieces of art. The guild is composed of local artists who are professional artists or who are emerging onto the professional art scene.

One of the primary missions of the gallery is that of an educational resource. Since the year 2000, the gallery has provided free guided tours to the area's youth. The gallery currently entertains about 1,000 school children each year. In addition to school children, many high level art students take advantage of the gallery for study and inspiration. The gallery currently works closely with several area art schools and their students.

Recently the gallery has been increasing their community interaction through the founding of the Friends of the Gallery. This group seeks input from members of the community about the needs they would like the gallery to meet. Because of the organization special events are now common. Lectures, workshops, classes, and instruction are all offered to the community on a regular basis.

The Union Street Gallery is open from noon until 4:00 p.m., Wednesday through Saturday.

Smith Museum of Stained Glass Windows

Navy Pier

600 East Grand Avenue

Chicago, IL 60611

321-595-5024

www.navypier.com

Free Admission Days: Always Free

The historic Navy Pier in Chicago is home to many fun activities for families to do. One of the most interesting things to do at the pier is to visit the Smith Museum of Stained Glass Windows. The museum is home to over 150 stained glass windows from a variety of time periods. Older windows at the museum date from the 1800's, whereas newer ones are from just a few years ago. The vast collection of stained glass windows includes works from artists such as Louis Comfort Tiffany, Roger Brown, and even Frank Lloyd Wright.

The 800 foot long museum is organized into various themed areas including Religions, Chicago-Art Nouveau, Prairie, Victorian Windows, and many other themes. One particular section of note contains stained glass windows from Chicago's 1893 World's Fair. Another collection of note is the *Richard H. Driehaus Collection.* This collection contains 13 windows which were created by Louis Comfort Tiffany. Everybody has their own favorites at the museum, but perhaps the most moving window is the American Flag 2001 window. The American Flag 2001 window was designed by artist Khaim Pinkhasik as a tribute to those who were touched by the attack of September 11, 2001.

The Smith Museum of Stained Glass Windows is open from 10:00 a.m. until 8:00 p.m., Sunday through Thursday. On Fridays and Saturdays the hours are from 10:00 a.m. to 10:00 p.m.

Illinois State Museum Chicago Gallery

James R. Thompson Center

Chicago, IL 60601

312-814-5322

www.museum.state.il.us/ismsites/chicago

Free Admission Days: Always Free

As part of its mission to provide access to all of its citizens, the Illinois State Museum operates a gallery within the confines of the immaculate James R. Thompson Center. The center opened in 1985 and provides visitors with a unique visual experience. Glass, marble, iron, and a 160 foot rotunda dominate this ultra-modern building. Visitors to the building will get the feeling that they have somehow been inserted into a futuristic science-fiction fantasy movie.

The gallery itself is located on the 2nd floor of the center. The gallery is home to a variety of artistic pieces in a variety of different mediums. Everything from paintings, to sculptures, to quilts has been displayed in the gallery. Exhibits change often so the gallery is a fine place to return to over and over. One program of note at the Illinois State Museum Chicago Gallery is the Arts in Architecture Program. The program has allowed the gallery to commission 19 works of art specifically for the museum. The program mandates that 0.5% of the money designated for construction of state-funded public buildings be used for the purchase of art.

Next to the gallery is the Illinois Artisans Shop. The shop specializes in handcrafted work from mid-western artists. Although it is a store, the shop also serves as an extension of the gallery which allows visitors to enjoy more than what they are able to see at the gallery.

Both the Illinois State Museum Chicago Gallery and the Illinois Artisans Shop are open from 9:00 a.m. until 5:00 p.m., Monday through Friday.

American Toby Jug Museum
910 Chicago Avenue
Evanston, IL 60202
877-862-9687
Free Admission Days: Always Free

Located in the basement floor of a new office building is the largest privately owned collection of Toby jugs in the world. Toby jugs are ale-cups which typically take the shape of a seated person wearing 18th century clothing. Toby jugs came into being around 1765, and it is said they were named after Squire Toby Philpot, a man with a renowned reputation for heavy drinking.

The earliest jugs normally featured jovial, heavy set, men, typically holding a pipe in one hand and a mug of ale in the other. As the art of Toby jug making evolved, more characters were added including some very unflattering depictions of women. As the centuries passed more popular characters were placed on jugs including, presidents, prime ministers, rock stars, and fictional TV characters. Currently the largest group of Toby jug purchasers consist of women aged 40 to 70, rather than the traditional male beer drinker.

At the American Toby Jug Museum there are over 6,000 Toby jugs which fill up about 100 display cases. Some of the jugs are very small, about an inch in height, while others are nearly three feet tall! All types of character mugs are available to view. Some of the more popular mugs include likenesses of the Beatles, Marilyn Monroe, and Ronald Reagan. The entire cast of Star Trek is also depicted on a series of mugs at the museum.

The museum is open to the public by appointment only, so be sure to call ahead.

The Chicago Cultural Center
78 East Washington Street
Chicago, IL 60602
312-744-3094
www.chicagoculturalcenter.org
Free Admission Days: Always Free

Known affectionately by the locals as the "People's Palace", the Chicago Cultural Center building has served the local citizens since 1897. The building was constructed to serve as Chicago's main library and was designed in the beaux-arts style. The building was designed by the architectural firm of Shepley, Rutan, & Coolidge. The architects sought inspiration from the Athens Acropolis, the Palazzo Vecchio of Florence, Italy, and the Doge's Palace in Venice. The most notable features of the building are its two stained glass domes, and the use of marble with inlaid mosaics.

The center, which cost over $2 million to build, stands at over 100 feet tall and consists of 5 stories. The outer walls of the structure are three feet thick and are faced with Bedford limestone. The inside of the building makes use of luxurious materials such as marble, Favrile glass, fine hardwood, mother-of-pearl, and colored stone. The dome at the south end of the building is considered to be the world's largest Tiffany style dome, with an estimated value of over $35 million. Because of its beauty, the center is a popular place for weddings, proms, formals, and high society soirées. In addition to all of these events, the Mayor commonly uses the center to entertain foreign Presidents and dignitaries.

In 1972, the building was listed on the National Register of Historic Places. In 1977, the building received a much needed makeover and in 1991, the building was rededicated as the Chicago Cultural Center upon the relocation of the City Library to the Harold Washington Library Center.

Today the building is divided into two theatres, two concert halls, eight galleries, a café, shop, dance studio, senior center, and a visitor's information center. The galleries contain a combination of rotating artworks as well as various items from the permanent collection. The galleries contain works from the whole spectrum of artistic media including: sculpture, paintings, crafts, architecture, and graphical art. The Landmark Chicago Gallery contains photographs which depict many of Chicago's early landmarks. Frequently the curators of the galleries set up special programs for school and youth groups to expose them to the world of art. The galleries are not the only things to see at the center though. The center offers dozens of musical performances monthly. The musical performances range from classical, to opera, to jazz, to avant-garde performances.

In addition to these many performances and galleries, locals like to use the center as a place to get out of the hustle and bustle of the city. Commonly locals can be seen lounging on the old armchairs and sofas which are scattered around the first floor. The center offers guided tours where visitors get to learn more about the history behind the center and its programs. These tours commonly start at 1:15 p.m., Wednesday through Saturday.

The building itself keeps long hours being open from 8:00 a.m. to 7:00 p.m., Monday through Thursday. On Friday the center closes at 6:00 p.m. Saturday's hours are 9:00 a.m. to 6:00 p.m., with Sunday's hours being 10:00 a.m. to 6:00 p.m. The center is closed on holidays.

Hyde Park Art Center

5020 South Cornell Avenue

Chicago, IL 60615

773-324-5520

www.hydeparkart.org

Free Admission Days: Always Free

Since 1939, the Hyde Park Art Center has served the city of Chicago as a focal point for alternative art. In addition to being a gallery space, the center has also been a focal point in the art education of the city's residents. Since 1940, the center has provided education through its School and Studio Program. The program consists of classes, workshops, camps, and outreach programs which serve students of all ages. Yearly over 4,000 area youths are also served by the program.

Along with the center's educational programs, the center also is home to the 4833 rph. The 4833 rph is a gallery space devoted to the display and discussion of creative works. Each month the gallery space hosts many interesting exhibitions and learning events. Budding artists and enthusiasts come together regularly to enjoy and discus art from various mediums. As part of the 4833 rph mission, often there are art shows which display art from all comers. These events give a rare opportunity to all artists to participate in full scale art exhibitions.

Not all of the art at the center is student or amateur art. The center hosts many exhibitions from well established visual artists. Many of the events focus on emerging professionals from the mid-west. Graduate student exhibitions are also hosted by the center.

The Hyde Park Art Center is open from 9:00 a.m. to 8:00 p.m., Monday through Thursday. Friday's and Saturday's hours are 9:00 a.m. to 5:00 p.m. On Sunday the center is open from noon to 5:00 p.m.

Lizzardo Museum of Lapidary Art

220 Cottage Hill

Elmhurst, IL 60126

630-833-1616

www.lizzadromuseum.org

Free Admission Days: Fridays Free

Making its home in Wilder Park, the Lizzardo Museum of Lapidary Art serves to display fine pieces of gemstone art. The term lapidary is defined as the art of cutting, polishing, and engraving gemstones. The art of lapidary has been around as long as people have roamed the earth. During the 1950's lapidary actually became a popular hobby in the U.S., with amateur artists producing volumes of fine jewelry.

Joseph Lizzardo was one of these lapidary artists. Joseph actually got his start in the lapidary arts in the late 1930's. Lizzardo specialized in working with jade, cutting and polishing it to his desired shape. Due to his love of lapidary art, Lizzardo decided to build a museum dedicated to his favorite hobby. With some of the fortune he had from his career at Meade Electric, Lizzardo built his museum, opening it in 1962. From that time, the museum has served to collect and display fine works of lapidary art.

Today the museum contains hundreds of pieces of art. Mosaics, bowls, vases, and figurines populate the museum. Special pieces from the collection include a Ming Dynasty alter set, and a gemstone encrusted screen. Dioramas are also present at the museum. Each diorama is a miniature recreation of a nature scene where the animals are carved from various gemstones.

The Lizzardo Museum is open from 10:00 a.m. to 5:00 p.m., Tuesday through Saturday. On Sunday the museum keeps hours of 1:00 p.m. to 5:00 p.m. In addition to the free Fridays, active military can view the museum free of charge any day it is open.

The Arts Club of Chicago
201 East Ontario Street
Chicago, IL 60611
312-787-3997
Attraction Free Days: Always Free

The Arts Club of Chicago has served a unique roll in the Chicago arts scene from its founding in 1916. Rather than focusing on the works of established masters, the Arts Club has sought to identify and display works from "tomorrow's masters". Throughout its many years, and many locations, the club has played host to dozens of exhibitions from artists who would eventually become household names. Artists like Picasso, Matisse, Salvadore Dali, and Jackson Pollock have had their early career shows at the club.

Along with the various exhibitions which have occurred, the club owns and displays many works from the new masters. Works from Picasso, Paul Klee, Henry Moore, and others make their home at the club. In addition to the collections, the club hosts lectures and musical performances. These lectures and performances are given by artists and performers who are considered to be fresh, cutting edge, and full of potential. Masters like Igor Stravinsky, William Butler Yeates, and Gertrude Stein have all visited the club to share their talents.

The Arts Club is housed in a 19,000 square foot building which was designed by John Vinci. The building is impressive in its interior design and its outdoor landscaping. The 1600 square foot garden compliments the brick exterior of the building and its white steel windows. The gallery at the club is open Monday through Friday from 11:00 a.m. to 6:00 p.m.

Smart Museum of Art

The University of Chicago

5550 South Greenwood Avenue

Chicago, IL 60637

http://smartmuseum.uchicago.edu

Free Admission Days: Always Free

In 1974, a museum was founded on the campus of the University of Chicago which serves to train artists, students, and teachers about the world of art. The early collection of the museum was composed of artworks which the university had collected throughout its long history. With the founding of the museum, the university was able to begin an organized campaign to build its collections.

Today the museum's collection contains a variety of paintings, drawings, sculptures, photographs, and even furniture. The 10,000 item collection contains works by noted artists like Mark Rothko, Frank Lloyd Wright, and H.C. Westerman. Works at the museum span over 5,000 years of history and include both Western and Eastern artworks. Throughout the year a variety of programs are held at the museum. Readings and concerts are among the most well attended of these events.

The museum also has a café and museum shop. Both the café and shop offer visitors an international experience through various foods and merchandise. The museum is open on Tuesdays, Wednesdays, and Fridays from 10:00 a.m. to 4:00 p.m. On Thursday the museum stays open until 8:00 p.m. Weekends the museum is open from 11:00 a.m. to 5:00 p.m.

Donald E. Stephens Museum of Hummels

5555 North River Road

Rosemont, IL 60018

847-692-4000

www.stephenshummelmuseum.com

Free Admission Days: Always Free

The story of the Donald E. Stephens Museum of Hummels begins in 1909 when Berta Hummel was born is Germany. Already a gifted artist, at the age of 18 she enrolled at the Munich Academy of Applied Arts. Throughout her time at the school she developed her craft as well as her sense of spirituality. Due to her growing faith, Hummel entered the Convent of Siessen after graduating in 1931. Fortunately, the convent was a place which had high regard for art and allowed Hummel to continue in her hobby.

After some time Hummel's artwork began to appear on postcards, and with permission from the convent, porcelain maker Franz Goebel began to produce 3-D figurines molded after Hummel's drawings. Tragically Hummel, now known by the name Sister I.M. Hummel, died at the age of 37. What didn't die was her artistic legacy. To this very day the Goebel Company is the sole producer of I.M. Hummel figurines. The company continues to produce new figurines, each approved by a board of directors from Hummel's old convent. Wildly popular with collectors, Hummels are on display at a variety of churches, people's homes, and museums.

The Donald E. Stephens Museum of Hummels currently contains the largest collection of publicly displayed Hummels in the world. The collection began in the 1960's when Stephens and his son were on a trip in Europe. From that time on the collection kept growing. In 1984, Stephens decided to donate his collection to the village to serve as a point of pride for the community.

Today the museum contains over 1,000 pieces, including a fine collection of ARNI figurines. The main difference between the Hummels and the ARNI figurines are the materials from which they are made. The Hummels are crafted from fine porcelain, whereas the ARNI figurines are carved from maple. Although the two types of figurines are carved from vastly different substances, they are similar in their beauty and subject.

The Donald E. Stephens Museum of Hummels is open to the public by appointment, so visitors are requested to call ahead. The museum is also home to a gift shop specializing in the sale of Hummels, Armani, Lladro, and Disney figurines.

Chicagoland Fun Fact

According to the U.S. Census Bureau, in the year 2000, 2.7% of Rosemont residents claimed Bulgarian ancestry. This tied Rosemont with Bowdon, Georgia for highest percentage of people claiming Bulgarian ancestry in the United States.

The Museum of Contemporary Photography

600 South Michigan Avenue

Chicago, IL 60605

312-663-5544

www.mocp.org

Free Admission Days: Always Free

As a project of Columbia College, The Museum of Contemporary Photography serves to feature photographic works from the 1940's to the present day. The museum's roots took hold upon the founding of the Chicago Center for Contemporary Photography in 1976. In 1984, a reorganization led to the founding of the current museum.

The first floor museum boasts a collection of over 700 works from American photographers. A great number of the photographs are of a commercial and artistic nature. Photographs which depict moments of social importance are also featured at the museum. One unique project that the museum has undertaken is *The Midwest Photographers Project* which seeks to feature works by mid-western photographers. Images which depict mid-western subjects and locations take precedence in this collection.

Annually the museum also presents traveling works from well known photographers. Each piece, on display at the museum, is well labeled with information about the image as well as the artist. The highly regarded photography department at Columbia uses the museum as a source of inspiration for their current students.

The first floor gallery keeps hours of 10:00 a.m. to 5:00 pm., Monday through Saturday. Sunday's hours are noon to 5:00 p.m. On Thursday the museum actually keeps its doors open until 8:00 p.m.

NATURE DAYS

Notebaert Nature Museum

2430 North Cannon Drive

Chicago, IL 60614

773-755-5100

www.naturemuseum.org

Free Admission Days: Thursdays Free

From 1857, the Chicago Academy of Sciences has strived to educate the people of Chicago about their environment. From its first days the academy has been collecting and displaying various artifacts and specimens dealing with nature and human's effect on the environment. In 1999, the academy took its largest step ever by opening the Peggy Notebaert Nature Museum.

The Peggy Notebaert Nature Museum is one of the largest nature museums in the world. With over 250,000 specimens in its collection, the museum strives to be a research center and an inspiring place for today's youth. One unique aspect of the specimen collection is the fact that many of the species represented are now extinct. Fortunately there is much life at the museum, especially in the visitor favorite Judy Istock Butterfly Haven.

The Judy Istock Butterfly Haven is a 2,700 square foot greenhouse which is home to over 250 species of butterflies. On any given day visitors have the opportunity to view some 75 species. Butterflies from all over the world are represented. Asia, Africa, North America, South America, and Australia are represented in the collection. If there were butterflies in Antarctica the haven would have them too! The main reason for the bounty of butterflies is the 1,000 chrysalides that are delivered to the museum weekly. Visitors to the Butterfly Haven get to learn about the life cycle, migration, and habits of various butterfly species. Butterflies are not the only things flying around the haven though. Colorful birds, four pairs, also make their home at the haven.

One of the hardest hitting exhibits at the museum is the Extreme Green House. The full sized house is located at the center of the museum. The house serves as a learning lab and explains the impact of human households on the environment. Things such as the relationship between eating fast food and the environment are illustrated in the Green House. Lessons in food borne bacteria, microbes, recycling, and composting are taught in the house. Visitors also learn how they can make eco-friendly household cleaners at home.

For those who want to walk through nature, the Wilderness Walk provides just that experience. The Wilderness Walk re-creates three distinct environments, dune, savanna, and prairie. Bison, deer, reptiles, and even a live ant farm can be seen. The Wilderness Walk allows the viewer to experience the sights and sounds that are typical of the mid-western region. Marshes are also common in the mid-west and the *Mysteries of the Marsh* exhibit covers the development and impact of mid-western wetlands.

Perhaps the most noticeable exhibit at the museum is the *Greening Project*. The project consists of 17,000 square feet of rooftop gardens. The gardens include a three-story cliff garden, a reflecting pool, and climbing vines. The project also seeks to minimize the environmental impact of the museum as a whole. The *Greening Project* makes use of solar panels, rainwater collection, and trees for cooling and air purification. By observing the *Greening Project* visitors can learn how they can use green technology to save energy at home.

The Peggy Notebaert Nature Museum is open Monday through Friday from 9:00 a.m. to 4:30 p.m. On weekends the hours are 10:00 a.m. to 5:00 p.m. The museum is open every day of the year with the exception of New Year's Day, Thanksgiving, and Christmas.

Sand Ridge Nature Center

15890 Paxton Avenue

South Holland, IL 60473

708-868-0606

www.fpdcc.com

Free Admission Days: Always Free

Thousands of years ago the area, which is now the home of the Sand Ridge Nature Center, was submerged under 40 feet of water. Lake Chicago covered an area larger than that of today's Lake Michigan. The result of the motion of the water was a relatively sandy area plentiful with smooth polished stone pebbles. Although Lake Chicago is no more, there is still water on the 235 acre preserve. Wetlands, trails, woodlands, sandy areas, and prairies fill the land which used to house a large farm.

Unfortunately for the farmers of the area, the land was not well suited for farming and was better for growing trees. Today a large variety of oak trees still grow on the park's grounds. The trees help to provide shelter for various migratory birds that rest at the park. Although the center is not conducive to commercial farming, the area does support several themed gardens for visitors to enjoy. During the summer the area is plentiful with butterflies and dragonflies. Many flowers are also in bloom each summer.

The Nature Center has a main building which houses exhibits on the people and wildlife of the area. Built in 1962, and expanded in 1992, the main building houses interpretive exhibits, hands-on activities, and many samples of small animals and reptiles. The Nature Center is open from March through October from 8:00 a.m. to 5:00 p.m. daily.

Kline Creek Farm/Timber Ridge Forest Preserve

County Farm Road

Wheaton, IL 60187

630-876-5900

http://dupageforest.com/education/klinecreek.html

Free Admission Days: Always Free

At over 1,100 combined acres, the Kline Creek Farm and Timber Ridge Forest Preserve provide visitors with many hours of enjoyment. The Kline Creek Farm takes up about 200 acres of the complex. The farm is operated by the Forest Preserve District of DuPage County as a learning tool for local citizens. The farm was purchased by the county in 1960 and opened to the public in 1984. At first the farm was only open for special events, but in 1989 the farm was opened to the public full-time. The farm, which began in the 1830's, has been restored to reflect how farming life was during the 1800's.

The typical farming activities of the 1800's can be viewed as visitors stroll the grounds of the farm. There are acres of row crops such as corn, wheat, and beans. Pastures for horses, sheep, and cattle are also abundant. Today the farm actively raises chicken, sheep, and cattle. An orchard and demonstration gardens allow visitors to see a variety of heirloom quality fruits and vegetables being grown and harvested.

In addition to all of the plants and animals, several buildings are available to see. The Farmhouse serves as the primary attraction. The Summer Kitchen is located near the house also. The Summer Kitchen is where the canning and processing of the newly grown crops took place. Due to the heat required for the canning process, people of the era would have a separate kitchen building so as not to heat up the house during an already warm summer. Standing nearby the Summer Kitchen is the Smokehouse where meat would be dried for preservation.

Throughout the year the farm hosts a variety of demonstrations and activities. Some of the more popular activities include sugar maple sugaring, canning, harvesting, haying, holiday celebrations, mock funerals, and mock weddings.

Just outside the grounds of the farm is the Timber Ridge Forest Preserve. The preserve, encompassing around 800 acres, serves to preserve trees and plants indigenous to the area. In addition to preserving plants and trees, the preserve also serves as a home for many different animals. Animals such as chickadees, beaver, herons, and mink all call the preserve home.

One unique feature of the preserve is its Spring Lake. The five-foot-deep lake serves as a habitat for a variety of plants and animals. Turtles, killdeer, and green frogs are plentiful at the lake. Plant species such as knotweed, bur reed, and white water lilies can also be seen.

One of the main activities at the preserve is hiking. The preserve includes over five miles of hiking trails. These trails are maintained well enough to allow for hiking, bicycling, horseback riding, and winter cross-country skiing. The trail system connects the preserve to the popular Illinois Prairie Path which consists of about 61 miles of trails spanning the entirety of DuPage County, as well as parts of Kane and Cook counties.

Both the farm and nature preserve are open year round. Normal operating hours for the farm are 9:00 a.m. to 5:00 p.m. The farm is closed on holidays. The nature preserve is open from one hour after sunrise to one hour after sunset.

Spring Valley Nature Sanctuary

1111 East Schaumburg Road

Schaumburg, IL 60194

847-985-2100

www.parkfun.com/dir/spv/index.html

Free Admission Days: Always Free

Schaumburg is home to a sanctuary of over 135 acres dedicated to
preserving the flora and fauna of northeastern Illinois. The Spring
Valley Nature Sanctuary is actually the home of five distinct preservation
attractions. The Bob Link Arboretum, Merkle Log Cabin, Volkening
Heritage Farm, Illinois Heritage Grove, and the Vera Meineke Nature
Center are all located within the acreage of the preserve.

Winding throughout the sanctuary are over three miles of trails, most of
which are handicap accessible. While strolling the trails visitors are able
to see many varieties of trees, birds, and small woodland animals. The
sanctuary is a popular place for bird watching, as well as amateur
photography.

With all of the unique attractions within the sanctuary, a variety of
educational activities are always available. At the Volkening Heritage
Farm visitors get to see what rural life was like in 1880's Illinois. The
Illinois Heritage Grove is complete with a collection of Illinois trees,
each labeled for easy identification. The Vera Meineke Nature Center
has a variety of exhibits which detail the natural history of the area. The
highpoint of the nature center is the habitat room which contains a turtle
and frog pond.

The different attractions within the Spring Valley Nature Sanctuary keep
different hours, which vary by season. The grounds and trails of the
sanctuary are open from 8:00 a.m. until 8:00 p.m. during the summer
season (April 1 through October 31). During the winter season
(November 1 through March 31) the hours are from 8:00 a.m. until 5:00
p.m.

Lake Catherine Nature Center and Botanic Gardens
7402 West Lake Katherine Drive
Palos Heights, IL 60463
708-361-1873
http://www.palosheights.org
Free Admission Days: Always Free

The Lake Catherine Nature Center and Botanic Gardens serves the area of Palos Heights as an example what can be done to beautify an area which has become an eyesore. In 1985, work began to restore the channel area which had been neglected for years. Through the efforts of local citizens, Trinity Christian College, and the University of Illinois Extension Service, Lake Katherine has become an award winning beacon of beauty for the area. Today the area is home to animals such as herons, ducks, geese, egrets, and beavers. A variety of trees and plant life also make their home at the preserve.

Master gardeners work diligently to tend to the many gardens present at the preserve. Wildflower gardens, herb gardens, a hosta garden, conifer garden, and vegetable garden dot the landscape of the preserve. Non-traditional gardens such as the Butterfly Garden, Rock Garden, and Waterfall Gardens can also be enjoyed at the preserve. In addition to the formal gardens, several non-formal growing areas exist. The Buzz 'N Bloom Prairie, and the Loretta Kupchick Woodland Wildflower Garden boardwalk are two examples of the non-traditional gardens at the preserve.

In addition to the gardens, several miles of trails exist at the preserve. Many hours can be spent walking on trails which range from 1/4 mile long all the way up to two miles. In addition to the outdoor activities, the Environmental Learning Center (ELC) offers many themed learning programs and activities. The ELC is open from 8:30 a.m. to 5:00 p.m., Monday through Friday. On Saturday the ELC is open from 8:30 a.m. until 4:00 p.m. The park itself has more extensive hours which vary by season.

Fullersburg Woods

3609 Spring Road

Oak Brook, IL 60523

630-850-8110

Free Admission Days: Always Free

In the community of Oak Brook there are over 200 acres dedicated to the preservation of the natural resources of the area. The Fullersburg Woods was opened to the public in 1920 and was named for early settler Benjamin Fuller, who arrived in the area in the 1830's. Fuller actually was responsible for forming the town of Fullersburg, which would later become the modern day Oak Brook. Throughout the years the Fullersburg Woods has been home to much activity. During the Great Depression the Civilian Conservation Corps (CCC) built many structures at the woods. Some of the structures included camps, the visitor's center, and picnic shelters. Over the years the woods became so popular that the human influence was starting to damage the landscape. The wear and tear on the environment became so bad that in the late 60's and early 70's several activities, such as picnicking and boating, were prohibited.

During the 1970's a prairie was restored which has continued to draw many songbirds to the park. Today the park boasts of several miles of trails, a fishing area, wildflower trail, mill, an interpretive trail, and a visitor's center. The visitor's center contains several exhibits including the remains of a woolly mammoth dating from over 13,000 years ago. Exhibits on animal tracks, bird spotting, and the Salt Creek are also present at the center.

The visitor's center at the Fullersburg Woods is open from 9:00 a.m. to 5:00 p.m. daily.

Phillips Park Zoo

1000 Ray Moses Drive

Aurora, IL 60505

630-978-4700

www.aurora-il.org/ParksAndRecreation/MunicipalParks

Free Admission Days: Always Free

Located in Aurora is a zoo which specializes in the collection of animals which are indigenous to North America. The Phillips Park Zoo has been moving forward in their mission for over 90 years. Over the years many animals have been added to the zoo. Those animals added include: otters, wolves, elk, llamas, and peacocks to name just a few. Many animals have actually been acquired by the zoo through various animal rescue efforts.

The facility does more than supply a comfortable home to rescued animals. The zoo provides a rich learning environment to the community and its guests. One special feature of the zoo is the sunken gardens. This feature is very popular with hobbyist photographers. There are plenty of walking paths, picnic spots, and a clean and safe shady playground. The zoo is definitely a great experience for younger children, but even older children and adults will have a good time.

The zoo has long hours being open from 9:00 a.m. to 8:00 p.m. daily (between Memorial Day and Labor Day). During the "off season" the zoo is open from 9:00 a.m. to 5:00 p.m. Additionally the zoo is open every day except Christmas Day and New Year's Day.

Chicago Botanic Garden

1000 Lake Cook Road

Glencoe, IL 60022

847-835-5440

www.chicagobotanic.org

Free Admission Days: Always Free

Located just north of the city of Chicago is the home of the Chicago
Botanic Garden. The Chicago Botanic Garden is a 385 acre collection of
gardens, woodlands, and habitats. The Chicago Botanic Garden's
existence can be traced back to the 1890 founding of the Chicago
Horticultural Society. The early years of the society were spent
supporting a variety of Chicago park initiatives. As time went on the
society faded away, but it was reborn in 1943.

Twenty years into its second life, the society was given control of 300
acres of forest at the garden's current location. From 1965 to 1972, the
society readied the land, transforming it into a series of gardens and
habitats for people to enjoy. From the 1972 opening, to the present day,
the garden has continued to evolve. Today the garden contains three
individual native habitats, as well as 23 display gardens. Notable features
of the Chicago Botanic Garden include: the Bonsai Collection, Dwarf
Conifer Garden, Japanese Garden, Aquatic Garden, and the Rose
Garden, among many others.

The garden is also a friendly stop for bicyclists although there is a slow 8
M.P.H. speed limit for cyclists. The garden also is home to a green house,
a tram, and a café. The garden is open from 8:00 a.m. to sunset during
the summer. Please note that parking fees are pretty steep at the
Chicago Botanic Garden, starting at $15 per car.

Willowbrook Wildlife Center
525 S. Park Boulevard
Glen Ellyn, IL 60187
630-933-7200
www.willowbrookwildlife.org
Free Admission Days: Always Free

Located in Glen Ellyn is a center devoted to the rescue and rehabilitation of the wild animals of DuPage County. The wildlife center was opened in 1952, and for almost 30 years its sole purpose was to treat wild animals that were injured due to human contact. In 1981, an outdoor exhibit, educational center, and treatment area were added. Today the center continues its mission of treating local animals in an effort to return them to their natural habitats.

One unique aspect of the Willowbrook Wildlife Center is the fact that they only rehabilitate local animals. There are no exotic species of animals at the center. Each year thousands of native animals are rehabilitated at the center. Unfortunately there are some animals so badly injured that they cannot be returned to their native habitats. These animals with permanent disabilities often become part of the center's outdoor exhibit. Native foxes, birds, raccoons, and opossums make their permanent residence at the center.

In addition to the rehabilitation efforts, and the permanent residents, the 50 acre center also serves as a nature sanctuary. Walking trails, the Butterfly Garden, and picnic areas stretch across the landscape. The Butterfly Garden is among the most popular spots at the center. The garden is home to many butterfly appealing flowers and plants. There is also a pond with trickling water to lure the butterflies. The garden serves as an example of the type of butterfly friendly landscaping that can easily be incorporated into suburban backyards.

In addition to all of the things to see outside, the center contains many indoor sights as well. Indoors the center contains a nursery, center information area, gift shop, and an interactive education area. In the education area there are many hands-on activities which allow visitors to learn more about the center and the animals it serves.

Throughout the year the center hosts a variety of educational and entertaining events. Nature hikes, birding events, and historical events are all held at the center. On occasion there are also "baby showers" which are held in honor of animals who are born at the center.

The Willowbrook Wildlife Center is open from 9:00 a.m. to 5:00 p.m. daily and is closed on holidays.

Chicagoland Fun Fact

Glen Ellyn was not always known as Glen Ellyn. Former names of the community include: Babcock's Grove, Dupage Center, Stacy's Corners, Newton's Station, Danby, and Prospect Park.

Plum Creek Nature Center/Goodenow Grove

27064 South Dutton Road

Beecher, IL 60401

708-946-2216

www.fpdwc.org/plumcreek.cfm

Free Admission Days: Always Free

Together the Plum Creek Nature Center and Goodenow Grove provide visitors with many fun and educational opportunities. The Goodenow Grove is a 689 acre preserve consisting of mostly oak-hickory forests. Within the acreage there are several grasslands and hills which increase the beauty of the area. The grove provides a home to many varieties of birds, deer, and various woodland creatures. Among the more common wild animals living in the grove are cardinals, owls, snakes, dragonflies, and butterflies.

As visitors walk the more than four miles of trails they can get a real sense of the wild beauty at the preserve. Unlike many preserves, during the winter the grove really comes alive. Winter hiking, cross country skiing, ice skating, and sledding are all popular activities at the site. It is very common for there to be 1,000 kids sledding on a cold winter weekend day. People are encouraged to bring their own sleds, although the nature center does rent out inner-tubes for about a dollar.

The Plum Creek Nature Center serves the grove as a warming up spot during the winter, as well as an educational resource year round. The center is complete with reading materials, coffee, hot water, bathrooms, a Discovery Den, and the Earth Care Center. The Discovery Den provides children with the opportunity to touch many nature artifacts and look at specimens under a microscope. For the more mature crowd the Earth Care Center offers grown-up displays on phenomena such as acid rain and landfill issues.

The Plum Creek Nature Center is open from 10:00 a.m. to 4:00 p.m., Tuesday through Saturday. On Sundays the center is open from noon until 4:00 p.m.

Chicagoland Fun Fact

The village of Beecher was named for the famous 19th century preacher Henry Ward Beecher. Although Rev. Beecher was reportedly aware of the founding of the new town, he chose not to attend the town's official dedication.

The Grove

1421 Milwaukee Avenue

Glenview, IL 60025

847-299-6096

www.glenviewparkdist.org/fa-grove-grounds.htm

Free Admission Days: Always Free

During the 1830's Dr. John Kennicott decided to relocate from New
Orleans to the area which currently makes up The Grove. Dr. Kennicott
was a well respected physician and horticulturalist who spent much of his
free time beautifying his property with plants and shrubbery. Today the
memory of Dr. Kennicott, as well as his horticultural legacy, lives on at
The Grove.

Today The Grove consists of 124 acres devoted to both historical and
natural preservation. The Grove is home to several historical and
educational sites. The Grove also serves as a home to many birds,
snakes, and woodland creatures. Winding throughout The Grove are
over two miles of walking trails which enable visitors to enjoy the beauty
of the area. Some of the features of The Grove include the Wetland
Greenhouse, Native American Village, Log Cabin, Interpretive Center,
The Grove Schoolhouse, and the Kennicott House.

The Wetland Greenhouse is open year round and provides a home for
various wetland creatures. Vintage fish tanks, colossal ferns, frogs,
crayfish, and a rain chamber can all be seen at the greenhouse. Around
the greenhouse a wetland has been created. The mission of the
greenhouse, and surrounding wetland, is to provide an educational
resource for those who want to know more about wetlands and their
preservation.

A ways down from the greenhouse is the Log Cabin and Native
American Village. Both the cabin and the village serve to recreate typical
dwellings of earlier settlers and the native peoples of the area. The

buildings are constructed using traditional techniques and contain traditional decorations and furnishings. The Native American Village has the Longhouse which is complete with a fire pit, fur covered bunks, and antlers used for decoration. A Tipi is also located in the Native American Village.

The Interpretive Center acts as a nature center and as the starting point for any visit to The Grove. The center is home to live animals, exhibits, and historical research items. The Interpretive Center was built in 1989, and was designed to compliment the buildings and woodlands of The Grove. The Interpretive Center hosts a variety of programs, displays, and classes all aimed at sharing knowledge of history and nature with its visitors.

The jewel of The Grove is the Kennicott House. The home, which was built in 1856, served as the domicile for Dr. Kennicott and his family. The exterior of the house has been restored to its original appearance, complete with rain barrels on the back porch. Special attention was paid to the interior of the home also. The home is filled with 19th century furnishings and decorations, most of which were owned by the Kennicott family. The home is open for tours on Sundays from February to September.

The Grove is open to the public from 8:00 a.m. to 4:30 p.m., Monday through Friday. On weekends the hours are 9:00 a.m. to 5:00 p.m. Like the Kennicott House, some of the buildings at The Grove keep different hours. However, the Wetland Greenhouse is open whenever The Grove is open.

The Lincoln Park Zoo

2001 N. Clark Street

Chicago, IL 60614

312-742-2000

www.lpzoo.com

Free Admission Days: Always Free

In 1868, the Lincoln Park Zoo was started with a collection of two swans. Over the years the zoo's collection has grown to over 1,200 animals. Today the Lincoln Park Zoo is actually comprised of several animal houses and mini-zoos. The mini-zoos are the Farm-in-a-Zoo and the Pritzker Family Children's Zoo. The focus of the mini-zoos is the education of the children of the Chicago area.

The Farm-in-a-Zoo is a project sponsored by John Deere, the makers of the famous green tractors and lawn mowers. The Farm-in-a-Zoo contains a large collection of animals that typically inhabit America 's farms. The goal of the Farm-in-a-Zoo is to expose city dwelling children to the agricultural lifestyle. One unique feature of the Farm-in-a-Zoo project is the fact that the dairy cows are milked publicly on a daily basis.

The Pritzker Family Children's Zoo is specifically designed for children. The Pritzker area contains an indoor area for children to explore. Up until recently the Children's Zoo was a petting area. Petting of the animals has been stopped due to health concerns. Even though the animals can no longer be touched, it is still possible to get up close with the animals. Many of the habitats are designed so that visitors will be eye to eye with the animals. Gorillas and giraffes especially enjoy making eye contact with their human guests. Other interesting areas of the zoo include the McCormick Bird House, Kovler Lion House, and the Antelope and Zebra Area.

The Lincoln Park Zoo is open 365 days per year and only closes during severe weather. Yearly over three million visitors make their way to this Chicago gem. The Lincoln Park Zoo also has the distinction of being the oldest public zoo in the country which does not charge admission. What the zoo does charge for is parking. Since the parking fee is pretty high, it is advised that you park somewhere else and ride the bus in from downtown. During the summertime a free trolley shuttles people between downtown and the zoo. Bringing a picnic lunch is always a good idea due to the ample opportunity for picnicking in the surrounding park land. Do allow up to two hours for your visit to the zoo, more time can easily be spent during special events such as their holiday light displays.

Chicagoland Fun Fact

In 1891 "The El," Chicago's first elevated railway, went into operation to begin the "Loop" that would circle the city's downtown area.

Bird Haven Greenhouse

225 North Cougar Road

Joliet, IL 60432

815-741-7278

www.jolietpark.org/facilities/greenhouse.shtml

Free Admission Days: Always Free

A very common location for weddings, the Bird Haven Greenhouse also serves the Joliet community as a repository of fine birds and plants. Since 1929, the greenhouse has hosted a variety of events, shows, and learning seminars for its visitors. The greenhouse was designed by the architectural firm of Lord and Burnham in the Italian Renaissance style. Surrounding the greenhouse are three beautiful acres of the conservatory. Within the conservatory grounds are many fine specimens which are used as a teaching tool for area youth.

Yearly over 200,000 people visit the greenhouse and conservatory. As a teaching tool many classes are held which serve to inspire young minds. The adjacent Barber & Oberwortmann Horticultural Center serves to spearhead the educational effort.

The Bird Haven Greenhouse is open year round. Each season is packed with floral shows, and each season begins a new motif within the glass walls of the greenhouse. Especially popular are the Desert House and the Tropical House. The Greenhouse is open everyday from 8:00 a.m. to 4:30 p.m.

Chicagoland Fun Fact

(Contributed by Adrianne Curry: Joliet native, actress, model, and co-star of VH-1's *My Fair Brady*)

"The Blues Brothers and Prison Break were both filmed at the famous Joliet Correctional Facility...closed down in 2004, I believe. It had the rep of being the baddest-ass prison in all the states."

Garfield Park Conservatory

300 North Central Park Avenue

Chicago, IL 60624

312-746-5100

www.garfield-conservatory.org

Free Admission Days: Always Free

In 1906, construction began on what would become one of the most impressive conservatories in the world. The 4.5 acre Garfield Park Conservatory was the result of a project spearheaded by Jens Jensen, the general superintendent and chief landscape architect of the West Park Commission. The complex was designed through the teamwork of architects, sculptors, metal workers, and artists. Their cooperation resulted in a still futuristic looking building which vaguely resembles a series of haystacks.

The conservatory complex is composed of six greenhouses, two exhibition halls, and a series of outdoor gardens. Inside the greenhouses are a series of themed areas, each concentrating on a specific field of plant rearing. For the indoor gardener the Aroid House offers many different types of houseplants to see. The main features of the Aroid House are the 16 glass lily pads crafted by renowned glass artist Chihuly.

The Desert House offers a much different view of the plant world. This greenhouse is filled with a variety of hot climate plants from small stone plants to large cactus plants. Aloe plants and even agave plants (the main ingredient for tequila) grow in the Desert House.

The Palm House exhibits plants which are commonly found in the most tropical of places. Palms, banana trees, and coconut palms all take advantage of the vaulted ceiling, growing tall in this greenhouse. The Double Coconut Palm, in the Palm House, is widely considered to be the largest one to be grown at a U.S. conservatory. Not all of the plants in the Palm House are tall, as many tropical flowers also call the Palm House home.

The Fern Room was designed to simulate the landscape of pre-historic Illinois. This was the goal of Jens Jensen, who helped design this "indoor swamp". Obviously ferns dominate this room, although they are not the normal house ferns which people are used to. Many of the ferns grow many feet tall. The oldest know plant species, the cycad, makes its home in the Fern Room.

Children will also find the conservatory fun, with the Children's Garden being the highlight of their day. The Children's Garden contains a variety of colorful plants for all to enjoy. The Children's Garden also has large size models of insects "flying" around. The Children's Garden is also designed to be an educational tool, with much information about the plants it contains readily available. Interactive displays are also present.

Children will also enjoy the Sweet House. The Sweet House aims to display plants which provide the goodies that everyone likes. Mangos, bananas, coconuts, figs, and cinnamon are all grown in the Sweet House. The parent plants for chocolate, chewing gum, and vanilla are also grown in the Sweet House.

In addition to the various houses, the conservatory contains two exhibition halls which host a variety of events each year. The outer grounds of the conservatory hold ponds, demonstration gardens, and even a garden inspired by the personal garden of Claude Monet.

The Garfield Park Conservatory is open daily from 9:00 a.m. to 5:00 p.m. On Thursdays the conservatory stays open until 8:00 p.m.

Wagner Farm

1510 Wagner Road

Glenview, IL 60025

847-657-1506

www.wagnerfarm.org

Free Admission Days: Always Free

Located in the village of Glenview is an area dedicated to the agricultural heritage of the area. Glenview itself, with over 45,000 residents, is more like a small city rather than a village. The well-to-do village has an extensive parks program as well as a variety of community building initiatives. With all of the efforts on community building, it is no surprise that the 18.6 acre farm exists today.

The farm itself is named for John and Catherine Wagner, German immigrants who arrived in the area in 1855. Being agricultural folks, they started their 100 acre farm to make their mark on the land. The farm was able to remain in the family for over 140 years, providing a living for several generations of Wagner descendents. In an effort to preserve the farm from development, the village purchased the site for use as an agricultural preservation center.

Currently the farm operates much like it did in its heyday. The farm has been restored and organized to operate in much the way a 1920's to 1950's farm would. It is during that time period that the field of agriculture became a lot more sophisticated. The 1920's brought about the beginning of several decades of innovation, industrialization, education, and improved product development. During these years the efficiency and yield of the average farm increased to near the level of today's farms.

At the farm visitors will be able to see how a real farm operates. There are milking demonstrations, interactive exhibits, equipment exhibits, and a greenhouse. In addition to the usual displays, there are a variety of programs and activities offered at the farm. Every Thursday at 4:00 p.m. there is a farm story time which is fun for the children. Being that Wagner Farm is a working farm, there are seasonal sales. Chrysanthemums, Pumpkins, and Christmas trees are all sold at the farm seasonally. The farm is also host to the Glenview Farmer's market where visitors can purchase the freshest produce direct from the grower. Bonfires, craft fairs, and festivals round out the yearly events at the farm.

The farm is open to the public from 1:00 p.m. to 5:00 p.m., Thursday through Sunday. During harvest times, and special events the farm is open additional hours.

Chicagoland Fun Fact

Glenview was home to Naval Air Station Glenview which served midwestern naval recruits as an anti-submarine training center. Some famous people who spent some of their military service at Glenview include: Neil Armstrong, Gerald Ford, George H.W. Bush, and Butch O'Hare.

Lincoln Park Conservatory

2391 North Stockton Drive

Chicago, IL 60614

312-742-7736

Free Admission Days: Always Free

In 1890, construction began on a conservatory which would replace a small greenhouse which was built 20 years earlier. The Lincoln Park Conservatory occupies about three acres and consists of an outside garden area, as well as a massive greenhouse structure divided into four display houses. The conservatory was designed by Joseph Lyman Silsbee with the assistance of M.E. Bell. The construction of the greenhouse was made possible by new advances in iron and glass construction. The construction of the conservatory took about five years, and to this day remains a testament to quality construction.

Today the greenhouse is home to many different species of plants and trees. Many of the plants and trees are native to tropical areas, but thrive here due to the constant humid 85 degree conditions within the greenhouse walls. Tropical ferns, palms, rubber trees, and orchids dominate the collection. So high is the quality of the specimens at the greenhouse, the Egyptian government requested seeds from the water lily collection in 1897. The greenhouse becomes a very popular destination for locals during the cold Chicago winters, and it is also a very popular first date location.

For those who want to learn more about the plants the greenhouse offers free guided tours on Fridays, Saturdays, and Sunday's. Tours of the greenhouse are lead by well trained guides who lead visitors around the facility discussing the history behind the greenhouse and each plant species it contains. For those who just want to look around or take photographs, the greenhouse can easily take over two hours to enjoy.

UNIQUELY
CHICAGOLAND

Marion E. Wade Center

Wheaton College

351 Lincoln Avenue

Wheaton, IL 60187

630-752-5908

www.wheaton.edu/wadecenter

Free Admission Days: Always Free

For over 40 years the Marion E. Wade Center has served Wheaton College, and the literary community, as a gathering place of works and artifacts from some of Britain's greatest authors. The center was started by English professor Dr. Clyde S. Kilby. Dr. Kilby had developed an ongoing correspondence with the famous author C.S. Lewis. Because of this ongoing communication, Dr. Kilby decided that a place dedicated to the seven great British authors should be created.

The result of Dr. Kilby's vision is the current Marion E. Wade Center. The center focuses on the works and lives of authors: Owen Barfield, George Macdonald, J.R.R. Tolkien, G.K. Chesterton, Charles Williams, Dorothy L. Sayers, and of course C.S. Lewis. The center is home to the museum, books, research materials, archives, photographs, videos, and various mementos. Large items at the center include bookcases belonging to Charles Williams, and a desk belonging to J.R.R. Tolkien.

Perhaps the most popular item at the center is the wardrobe which belonged to C.S. Lewis' grandparents. It is said that this wardrobe, currently filled with period fur coats, served as the inspiration for the classic book *The Lion, the Witch, and the Wardrobe*. The book has been re-popularized recently with the release of the film *The Chronicles of Narnia*. Those who wish to view the wardrobe will see a warning plaque which states, "Enter at your own risk. The Wade Center assumes no responsibility for persons who disappear or who are lost in this wardrobe".

Interestingly, the Wade Center has a close connection to another critically acclaimed movie. Actress Debra Winger came to the Wade Center to do research for the movie *Shadowlands*, which also starred Anthony Hopkins. The Oscar nominated *Shadowlands* tells the story of C.S. Lewis and his relationship with American author Joy Davidman Gresham.

Currently the Wade Center draws about 5,000 visitors each year. In addition to the exhibits and materials at the center, many informative programs are held each year. The center's regular hours of operation are 9:00 a.m. to 4:00 p.m., Monday through Friday. On Saturday the center is open from 9:00 a.m. until noon.

Chicagoland Fun Fact

Wheaton has the distinction of having the most churches, per capita, in the United States.

Chicago Children's Museum

700 East Grand Avenue

Chicago, IL 60611

312-527-1000

www.chicagochildrensmuseum.org

Free Admission Days: Varies

In 1982, the Junior League of Chicago formed the Chicago Children's Museum due to funding cuts in public school arts programs. The early years of the museum were spent in two hallways of the Chicago Public Library. After several years, and a few moves, the museum opened its present location in 1995. Today the three floor, 57,000 square foot site entertains over 1 million visitors each year. The Chicago Children's museum is the second most visited children's museum in the United States.

The museum contains a variety of hands on activities to enjoy. The special thing about the museum is the fact that many of the exhibits pertain to life in Chicago. There is the *Kids Town* exhibit in which children can change a tire, drive a CTA bus, and even shop. The exhibit actually takes the form of a miniature cityscape which teaches problem solving skills. The *Play it Safe* exhibit, which was designed with the help of the Chicago Fire Department, allows children to learn about fire safety as well as how to deal with common emergencies. Children will learn how to develop fire escape routes, how to be safe on the street, and they can even take the "Safety Patrol Pledge".

The two most unique exhibits at the museum are the *BIG Backyard* and the *Dinosaur Expedition*. Both of these exhibits are also very hands on. The *BIG Backyard* exhibit represents an urban garden, except for the fact that everything has been scaled up enough to tower over small children. Insects, plant, toadstools, and fantasy plants all "grow" at the exhibit. The *Dinosaur Expedition* is an actual recreation of a real expedition which took place in the Sahara desert back in 1997. On this expedition a new dinosaur species was discovered, the fish-eating Suchomimus. Children will have the chance to join in and actually take part in a mock dinosaur bone excavation.

The interactive exhibits continue with the museum's Inventing Lab. The Inventing Lab enables visitors to see things which were invented by Chicago-area students. There is also a Grand Piano Slide, and a two story tall tower in which to fly machines which can be invented at the museum. The Artabounds Gallery exhibits various artworks from families who have visited the museum.

The Chicago Children's Museum is open from 10:00 a.m. to 5:00 p.m., Sunday through Wednesday. From Thursday to Saturday the museum is open from 10:00 a.m. to 8:00 p.m. Major corporations sponsor free admission days, some for children and some for all, so be sure to check out the museum's web-site for times and dates.

Chicagoland Fun Fact

On October 7, 1997, Mrs. O'Leary's cow was officially absolved of all blame for the Great Chicago Fire by the Chicago City Council.

Elks National Veterans Memorial

2750 North Lakeview

Chicago, IL 60614

773-755-4876

www.elks.org/memorial

Free Admission Days: Always Free

In 1926, the Elks club built the Elks National Veterans Memorial as a tribute to all those who had fought for America's freedom. The Elks Club, more formally known as the Benevolent and Protective Order of Elks, was founded in 1868 by a group of New York City actors. Over the years people of other professions began to join.

Known largely as an organization which promotes patriotism, the Elks have over one million members today. One of the contributions the Elks made to American patriotism was the creation of Flag Day. Today the Elks National Veterans Memorial stands as an example of the Elks' commitment to national pride. Serving as the Elks' national headquarters, the building contains statues, paintings, a rotunda, and a grand reception room. The building was designed by Egerton Swarthout, and contains sculptures by James Earle Fraser, Laura Gardin Fraser, and Adolph A. Weinman. Murals painted by Eugene Savage and Edwin Blashfield also decorate the memorial. The combination of artwork and architecture fills visitors with wonder and appreciation.

The impressive Memorial Rotunda contains bronze statues representing the virtues of justice, charity, fidelity, and brotherly love. The rotunda stands 100 feet tall, from the floor to the top of the dome. The lower level of the rotunda contains many marble columns, each made with different granites, adding a variety of colors to the space. The floors are equally impressive with a series of squares and circles laid into the pinkish base rock. All the stone surfaces are polished to a mirror shine allowing light to bounce around the room. The upper level of the rotunda contains stained glass windows and a series of paintings which stretch around the circumference of the upper level. Marble columns of darker browns, greens, and reds separate each work of art. At the very top of the rotunda is the Grand Dome. The dome is constructed with a series of diamond and hexagon shapes all leading up to the light at the top. The colors teal, tan, brown, and gold make up the inner surface of the dome.

Perhaps more impressive than the Rotunda is the Grand Reception Room. The Grand Reception Room makes use of a variety of polished woods in an effort to impress. The room contains two large polished wood tables, fine sitting chairs, three colorful floor carpets, and a series of carved wooden columns. Murals adorn this room also stretching up to and onto the ceiling. Several beautiful chandeliers both decorate and supply light to the room. Lightning is also provided by the massive stained glass windows of the room.

In addition to the main rooms, the memorial also has a series of alcoves and nooks which contain a variety of interesting and beautiful features. The Elks National Veterans Memorial is open Monday through Friday, from 9:00 a.m. to 5:00 p.m.

Chicagoland Fun Fact

The first hospital in Illinois, Chicago's Mercy Hospital, was opened in 1863.

Millennium Park

201 E. Randolph Street

Chicago, IL 60614

312-742-1168

www.millenniumpark.org

Free Admission Days: Always Free

Although construction wouldn't begin until 1998, the idea for a park at
the Millennium Park location originally sprung up in 1977. At the time
there was little support and the idea eventually faded away for almost 20
years. With two decades of time passed, Mayor Daily proposed a park to
be built, this time with much support from the community. Large
businesses also supported the park to the tune of $145 million. The park
was officially dedicated in 2004, and holds a variety of treasures for its
visitors.

The first thing most visitors do at the park is stop by the welcome center.
The welcome center provides a variety of materials for visitors to better
enjoy the park. Free guided tours of the park also originate at the
welcome center. Guided tours start at 11:30 a.m. and 1:00 p.m. daily.
The tours run from late May to late October. For those who can't make
a tour time, the park offers a free downloadable MP3 audio tour on the
park's web-site. Both the physical tour and audio tour lead visitors
around the park and tell interesting details of what the park contains.

Many different gardens, fountains, and works of art decorate the park.
One of the most interesting features of the park is the Cloud Gate. This
piece of art was designed by Anish Kapoor. The sculpture is made of
polished stainless steel and weighs in at 110 tons. The sculpture is 66
feet long and 33 feet high. The sculpture features a 12 foot arch for
curious visitors to walk under and admire their reflection in the mirror
finish.

Not to be outdone, Jaume Plensa designed the Crown Fountain. This
fountain features two 50 foot glass block towers. Between the towers

sets a shallow reflecting pool. The most unique features of the fountain are the faces that are projected on the towers. The faces were part of a project by local art students. Photographed by the students, the faces are projected at random onto the towers. There are 1000 different faces that are projected on the towers and they change about every five minutes.

For the plant lover the park has plenty of growing plants to see. Yearly, plants are selected to add color and fragrance to the park. The Laurie Garden provides an abundant 2.5 acres of plant life to appreciate. The main feature of the garden is the 15 foot tall hedge. Known as the *Shoulder Hedge*, the hedge represents Carl Sandburg's description of Chicago as the "City of Big Shoulders".

The center point of the park is the Jay Pritzker Pavilion. The pavilion serves as an outdoor amphitheater, and host to many of Chicago's famous cultural events. The pavilion consists of a 4,000 seat outdoor concert hall, and a great lawn which can seat about 7,000. Every week the pavilion hosts a variety of acts from all genres of music. Most concerts are free and a schedule can be viewed at the web-site.

Next to the pavilion is the start of the BP Bridge. The 925 foot bridge serves the park as a link to the nearby Bicentennial Park. The bridge was built to offer crossers spectacular views of the city skyline as well as Lake Michigan. One unique feature of the bridge is the use of acoustic barriers to block out the sounds of Columbus Avenue.

Many additional treasures can be found in the park including the Millennium Monument, Chase Promenade, and the Boeing Galleries. During the winter there is an ice rink which is open to the public.

Millennium Park is open daily from 6:00 a.m. to 11:00 p.m. Unfortunately no non-service animals are allowed in the park.

Balzekas Museum of Lithuanian Culture
6500 South Pulaski Road
Chicago, IL 60629
773-582-6500
www.lithaz.org/museums/balzekas
Free Admission Days: Mondays Free

While Chicago is well known for having a large number of people of Polish decent, most people are not aware that the largest number of Lithuanian people, not currently living in Lithuania, also call Chicago their home. The Balzekas Museum of Lithuanian Culture celebrates the rich culture and history of the Lithuanian people. Auto dealer Stanley Balzekas, Jr. began the museum in a building adjacent to his car dealership back in 1966. The museum was stocked with items from his personal collection. Art work, armor, and maps made up the collection of the early museum. Eventually, the collection would expand requiring a new location.

In 1986, the museum moved into its current location, a former hospital! Throughout the years additional artifacts were gathered, making the museum the largest collection of Lithuanian artifacts to exist outside of Lithuania. Today the museum has a large volunteer staff along with several curators. The education of children is given priority in this museum with their special Children's Museum of Immigrant History. The museum offers a video which gives a good overview of Lithuanian history and images of the country.

The museum offers fun and education for the whole family with its many maps, paintings, weavings, and photos. Around Christmas and Easter the museum puts on special events which teach about the old country holiday traditions. The museum is also home to a fine collection of amber jewelry, a product for which Lithuania is well known. The museum is open daily from 10:00 a.m. to 4:00 p.m.

Grant Park

337 East Randolph Street

Chicago, IL 60601

312-742-7648

www.chicagoparkdistrict.com

Free Admission Days: Always Free

In 1835, the citizens of Chicago decided that there should be a place in the city forever spared from commercial development. What resulted from this decision was the formation of Grant Park, which is affectionately referred to as Chicago's "front yard". The park was officially dedicated in 1844, and was known as Lake Park. The park was actually able to grow in size due to the dumping of the debris from the Great Chicago Fire of 1871 into the lake. In 1901, Lake Park was renamed Grant Park to honor U.S. President, and war hero, Ulysses S. Grant.

Even though the original park was supposed to be free from development, many plans were made for construction on the park's lands. Fortunately, for the park today, Chicago businessman Montgomery A. Ward fought these efforts in court. In 1911, Ward earned final victory in a decision passed down by the Illinois State Supreme Court.

The park today is home to one of the most famous urban landmarks in the country, the Clarence Buckingham Fountain. The fountain was built under the direction of Kate Buckingham in 1927 as a tribute to her brother. The fountain's design was inspired by the great fountains of Europe, namely the *Bassin De Latome*. The fountain has four levels and 133 jets of water. The fountain's central jet shoots water over 150 feet high. Every hour, between 8:00 a.m. to 11:00 p.m., the fountain is programmed to perform a dazzling 20 minute water show. Nighttime is especially good due to the use of lights and music in the water show. New visitors to Chicago often find the fountain to be a familiar sight due to its use in the opening montage of the long running comedy *Married...With Children.*

Today the park consists of 319 acres dedicated to the enjoyment of its visitors. The park is complete with fields, trees, walking paths, and great views. For the sporting types, tennis courts, basketball courts, and 16 softball fields await. Free locker room facilities are located at the Bicentennial Plaza.

Annually the park hosts a variety of local and international events. The park has hosted events such as the Taste of Chicago, the Chicago Jazz Festival, Lollapalooza, and Mass with Pope John Paul II. The park was also the sight of the infamous riots at the 1968 Democratic National Convention.

Recently the park has been the beneficiary of a multi-million dollar "spruce up" effort. The park is open to the public 24 hours per day, year round.

Chicagoland Fun Fact
The first Rotary Club in America was founded in Chicago in 1905.

Swedish American Museum Center

5211 North Clark Street

Chicago, IL 60640

773-728-8111

http://samac.org/

Free Admission Days: Second Tuesday of Each Month

Surprisingly Chicago is home to the largest group of Swedish people in the world with the exception of Stockholm, the capitol city of Sweden. Because of this distinction Chicago is home to the Swedish American Museum Center. The center is devoted to the culture of Swedish Americans, as well as their history. So great is the influence of the center that it has been visited by the King of Sweden on two separate occasions.

The museum consists of three floors and 24,000 square feet dedicated to the life and culture of Swedes in America. Exhibits pertaining to the influx of Swedes into the Chicagoland area over 200 years ago are present. Information about the contributions that Swedish decedents have made to the new world is also present. Log cabins, zippers, and propellers were all introduced by Swedes. Art work is one of the main features of the museum. Several times per year the museum exhibits various artworks for Swedish artists, some well known, and others who are emerging.

The Children's Museum of Immigration provides an opportunity for children between ages three and twelve to learn what it was like for new immigrants coming to America. There is an old Swedish farmhouse, a Viking ship, an immigrant steamer, and a host of hands on activities. The Children's Museum is included within the center.

The Swedish American Museum Center is open from 10:00 a.m. to 4:00 p.m., Tuesday through Friday. On weekends the center is open from 11:00 a.m. until 4:00 p.m.

Harold Washington Library Center
400 South State Street
Chicago, IL 60606
312-747-4136
www.chipublib.org/001hwlc/001hwlc.html
Free Admission Days: Always Free

Since 1991, the Harold Washington Library Center has served the city of
Chicago as a collecting place for books, art, artifacts, and academic
resources for its citizens. The center's building consists of over 750,000
square feet and nine floors. The building is so large that it has appeared
in *The Guinness Book of World Records* as the world's largest public library
building. The building design was the result of a contest held in 1988,
with Thomas H. Beeby providing the winning concept. The building was
constructed in the neo-classical style. The building makes liberal use of
elements from both Greek and Roman architectural styles. Cast stone
ornamentation, granite blocks, and red brick give the building its strong
appearance. Glass is also featured on the exterior of the building through
the use of five story tall arched windows, and the Plymouth Court face
glass wall. Inside the building the neo-classical design continues. Arches,
vaulted ceilings, and columns are all abundant within the building.

Artwork is also abundant in the building, making the entire facility
essentially an art museum which happens to have books. Murals, statues,
paintings, and photographs decorate the many hallways and walls of the
center. On the second floor Chicago painters are featured through the
collection of artwork displayed in the walkway above the main lobby.
The sixth floor features two cannons from the Civil War. The eighth
floor is home to five of the non-winning architectural models from the
center's 1988 design contest. The eighth floor also houses the center's
collection of photographs, musical recordings, as well as piano and
chamber music practice rooms.

The visual highlight of the center is the ninth floor which houses the
Winter Garden. A skylight provides daylight for the olive trees which

make their home inside the center. Exhibit halls occupy the ninth floor providing much needed space for the artifacts which are held at the center.

Even though the center is stuffed full of art, its main purpose is that of a library. The center is home to a variety of unique collections of books, manuscripts, and audio files. One of the most unique collections of the center is housed in the Talking Book Center. The Talking Book Center provides over 50,000 books in Braille and recorded format. Through the Talking Book Center patrons also have access to a Computer Book Reader which is able to convert written text into spoken words; essentially it can read any book out loud for someone!

The newspaper and periodical section, on the third floor, has one of the most impressive selections of newspapers and magazines in the world. Over 300 different newspapers are represented in the collection. Papers from every state, and 24 foreign countries, are available for viewing. Perhaps the most impressive distinction of the section is the fact that every issue of the New York Times, The Times of London, and the Chicago Tribune ever printed is available on microfilm.

Programs for children are abundant at the center through the Thomas Hughes Children's Library. The Children's Library was actually named for British Parliamentarian Thomas Hughes. Hughes was responsible for organizing a book drive in England shortly after the Great Chicago Fire. Because of his tireless efforts, over 8,000 books were collected from almost every living English author. The books which were collected became the backbone for the new Chicago Public Library collection. Today the Children's Library operates much like an independent entity within the library, with its own circulation desk, programs, and book collection.

Throughout the rest of the facility patrons can get help with job searches, research projects, state law, patent searches, and education. The Harold Washington Library Center is open from 9:00 a.m. to 9:00 p.m., Monday through Thursday. On Friday and Saturday the hours are 9:00 a.m. to 5:00 p.m. Sunday's hours are from 1:00 p.m. to 5:00 p.m.

Chicagoland Fun Fact

New York Sun Editor Charles Dana dubbed Chicago the "Windy City" because she was tired of all of the bragging by Chicago residents associated with the city's hosting of the World's Columbian Exposition of 1893.

The Newberry Library

60 West Walton Street

Chicago, IL 60610

312-943-9090

www.newberry.org

Free Admission Days: Always Free

In 1841, Chicago businessman Walter Loomis Newberry came up with the idea of establishing a public library in the north section of Chicago. Before his death, Newberry stipulated in his will that a library would be created with use of his estate's assets after the passing of his wife and daughters. By the time his daughters and wife had passed on, the city had already established the full service Chicago Public Library. With this now being the case, the trustees of the Newberry estate decided to take a slightly different approach to Newberry's mission.

In 1887, the library began its operations as a privately funded public reference library. The library is unique in the fact that it is a non-circulating library. The library also does not have general reading books, movies, or the newest Stephen King novel. What the library does have is one of the best collections of humanities based volumes in the country. The library contains over 5 million pages of manuscripts, 1.5 million books, and 300,000 maps. The period of time from the middle ages to the 20th century are all represented at the library. As a research library, the library does not offer open browsing of the collection, but readers age 16 and older are allowed to use materials for research. The librarians are full service agents who assist in identifying the works which will best aid a person's research.

People of all ages are invited to take a free tour of the library. Tours often take place on Thursdays at 3:00 p.m., and Saturdays at 10:30 a.m. There is also a gallery which provides a variety of things to see.

The regular hours of the library are 10:00 a.m. until 6:00 p.m., Tuesday through Thursday, and 9:00 a.m. to 5:00 p.m. on Friday and Saturday.

The Jerry Springer Show
454 North Columbus Drive
Second Floor
Chicago, IL 60611
312-321-5365
www.jerryspringertv.com
Free Admission Days: Always Free

On September 20, 1991, one of the most controversial shows in television history aired for the first time. *The Jerry Springer Show* was actually conceived as a replacement for the well respected *Phil Donahue Show*. The early episodes of *The Jerry Springer Show* featured guests such as Oliver North, Jesse Jackson, and Sally Jesse Raphael. In the early shows guests debated the hot-button issues of the day like gun control and racism. Although the discussion of such issues was intelligent and dignified, the ratings for *The Jerry Springer Show* were disappointingly low. Without a fast, radical change the show would soon meet its end.

The person charged with rescuing *The Jerry Springer Show* from its low ratings was producer Richard Dominick. Dominick transformed *The Jerry Springer Show* from a highbrow political discussion show, to the raucous circus of dysfunction it is today. The show puts all of its assets into recruiting guests who engage in the highest level of deviant behavior. Most of the guests have a lower socioeconomic status than the average American, and the subjects of the shows are soapopraesque. So wild is the behavior of the guests, and the topics of the show, Jerry himself has referred to it as a "freak show". The show actually bills itself as "The Worst Show on Television".

Whatever people may think about the show, it has become a wildly popular American phenomenon. So popular is the show that back in the late 1990's, for a short time, *The Jerry Springer Show* enjoyed higher ratings than the *Oprah Winfrey Show*. The effect of *The Jerry Springer Show* has been profound on the television industry. Because of the show "trash TV" has become its own genre whose influence can be seen in everything from talk shows to judge's shows. The advent of "trash TV" has also led to the decline in the number of daytime game shows.

Before he was the host of his own show, Jerry Springer had a long career as a politician and journalist. Springer was a key player in the push for the 26th Amendment which lowered the voting age from 21 to 18. Springer also served as an aide to Senator Robert F. Kennedy. Springer's political career also included time as a Cincinnati City councilman and Mayor.

After Springer's failed bid for the Ohio Governorship he went into broadcasting. Springer was given his first opportunity on the low rated WLWT news program. In two short years Springer worked himself up to become the most popular news anchor in the city. Because of this distinction Springer was a multiple time Emmy award winner. Springer's real claim to fame, at that time, was his role as a political commentator. His views, which were shaped in part to his status as a British born Jewish immigrant, (his parents had fled to Britain from Germany prior to WWII) resonated with the people of the Cincinnati area.

In 2006, *The Jerry Springer Show* celebrated its 3000th episode. Due *The Jerry Springer Show's* success, a spin off show was created for Jerry Springer's longtime security manager Steve Wilkos. Tickets to the show are free and are available by calling (312) 321-5365, or by visiting the Jerry Springer web-site. Children are not allowed to attend tapings due to the adult nature of the shows. If you are not familiar with the show do watch an episode on TV to make sure you would really like to see the craziness in person.

Chicago Bears Training Camp
Olivet Nazarene University
One University Avenue
Bourbonnais, IL 60901
815-35-BEARS
www.bearstrainingcamp.info
Free Admission Days: Always Free

Since 1921, the Chicago Bears have represented the city of Chicago at the highest levels of professional football in the land. The team was actually founded in 1919 as the Decatur Staleys, a company team of the A.E. Staley Company. In 1921, the team was relocated to Chicago and became a charter member of the new NFL. Today only two of the original teams remain, those being the Bears and the Arizona Cardinals (formerly the Chicago/Racine Cardinals then St. Louis Cardinals). In 1922, the team was renamed the Bears, and has been know for their tough gritty play ever since.

For their first few decades NFL championships for the Bears were a very common occurrence. The Bears dominated their competition many years winning an astounding 8 NFL championships. Most of these championships came in the 1930's and 1940's as the team was almost unstoppable. In 1970, the NFL merged with the American Football League (AFL) forming a new unified NFL. Because of the increased competition, even with future legends Walter Payton and Dick Butkus on the field, it would take until the mid 1980's for the Bears to regain championship form.

When the Bears returned to championship form they did so with avengeance. Starting in 1984, the Bears dominated their division winning it five straight years from 1984 through 1988. For good measure they also added another division title in 1990. During this period the Bears were known for their punishing defense, colorful personalities, and their singing. That's right, their singing! As a publicity stunt during their

1985 championship season the Bears released a hit song and video, *We are the Bears* A.K.A. *The Superbowl Shuffle*. The group rap featured all of the players rapping about dominating the football field. The tune really caught on reaching #41 on the Billboard Top 100. In addition to chart success, the video earned much airplay on a young cable channel known as MTV.

The Bears of that year could do more than just rap about football, they could play. The team that year finished the regular season with only a single loss. The playoffs were a breeze for the Bears as they easily dispatched the New York Giants and L.A. Rams a combined 45-0. Only the wild card New England Patriots could stand between the Bears and the Superbowl 20 victory. Ironically the Superbowl victory would be the Bear's easiest as they were able to get a quick lead on the speedy Patriots. The Bears used a punishing defense, as well as some offensive trickery to take the Patriots out of the game early. Perhaps the most well known play is when the over 300 lb. William "The Refrigerator" Perry was used as a running back, bowling over the Patriot defense to score an easy early touchdown. After such a dominating performance the Bears were expected to win many Superbowls. Although they dominated their division for some years they would not qualify for another Superbowl until the 2006 season.

Prior to each season the Bears have their annual training camp at Olivet Nazarene University. The purpose of the training camp is to allow the older players to get into shape while allowing younger players the opportunity to make the football team. The training is a very family friendly event and usually runs from late July until mid-August. Commonly players are willing to sign autographs for fans, particularly some of the up-and-coming players. The whole experience allows fans to see what football practice is really like, and the effort it takes to craft a winning team.

Information for the training camp can be accessed best through the web-site, as well as calling 815-35-BEARS. The local paper the *Daily Journal* is a good resource for camp information as well as autographable posters.

Downers Grove Plowboys Vintage Baseball Club

4435 Middaugh Avenue

Downers Grove, IL 60515

630-719-5810

www.dgplowboys.com/Home.htm

Free Admission Days: Always Free

Back in the 1800's baseball was truly America's national pass-time. Back then towns of every size were represented by a team, and many sunny afternoons were filled with the sound of the crack of the bat, cheers from fans, and the calls of vendors selling refreshments to the audience. The rules of that old game were significantly different than the rules of today. Back then rules even varied from town to town, making it necessary for the managers to meet and agree on a distinct rule set for each and every game. Even though the rules differed by location some rules were fairly constant.

Perhaps the largest difference between the vintage game and the game of today is the role of the pitcher. Back in the early days of baseball the pitcher was obligated to pitch a hittable ball over home plate. There were no sliders, fastballs, spit balls, or knuckleballs in the olden days. In some leagues the batter was even allowed to instruct the opposing pitcher exactly where they would like the ball pitched to them. Fly balls were also different. Today if a batter hits a ball, and the fielder catches it before it hits the ground, the batter is out. In vintage days the ball could bounce up to one time before the fielder caught it, and the batter would still be out. In the past catchers would be positioned a few feet behind the batter and catch the pitchers throw "off the bounce". Today, of course, the catcher snags the pitcher's 90 M.P.H. pitch directly out of mid-air. The speed of today's game made necessary the trend of fielders wearing gloves. The slower game of yesteryear found most fielders playing without gloves.

As the game of baseball evolved the local teams were replaced by well organized minor league teams. The larger cities started to sponsor major professional teams leading to the near extinction of adult amateur baseball. During the 1980's, ironically when professional baseball was arguably at its peak as the major American sport, amateur teams started to spring up across the countryside. These amateur teams went so far as to adopt the old rules and customs of the game. The phenomenon started in the 1980's is now referred to as vintage baseball.

As people have become more jaded by the goings on in professional sports, the vintage game has flourished. Currently there are dozens of leagues and several national governing bodies. The vintage games of today are an approximation of the games of yore, due to the fact that there are thousands of variations of rules between clubs. Today the vintage managers again meet before games to lay down the ground rules of the day. Today the trend in vintage baseball is to use rules, uniforms, and strategies which were common for the period of the mid to late 1800's.

In 2004, a group of men held a test game in Downers Grove and so was reborn the vintage game in the community. Such a good time was had that in 2006 the Downers Grove Plowboys Vintage Baseball Club was officially formed. The Plowboys were named for a local political group of the 1850's era. Legend has it that the men of the political group would spend their time between campaigns playing baseball against rival groups from the Chicago area. Today the modern Plowboys are all about baseball. The team currently travels across the Midwest in search of vintage baseball matches. The active team plays upwards of 25 plus games per year, including an active home schedule.

Home games for the Plowboys are always free, and visitors are actively encouraged to attend. All games take place at the Herrick Middle School Ball Field. A complete schedule is available at the Plowboys web-site. More information about the Plowboys, and the community of Downers Grove, can be obtained from the Downers Grove Museum. The museum, located at 831 Maple Avenue, is open to the public Sunday through Friday from 1:00 p.m. to 3:00 p.m. Admission to the museum is also always free.

Oprah Winfrey Show

Harpo Studios

1058 West Washington

Chicago, IL 60607

312-591-9222

www.oprah.com

Free Admission Days: Always Free

Oprah, everybody knows who she is. She is one of the few figures in
America whose popularity spans across almost every ethnic, economic,
and gender group. Having amassed a billion dollar fortune it is hard to
believe that Oprah Winfrey was born into very modest beginnings.
Oprah was born in 1954, in Kosciusko, Mississippi to parents who were
teenagers living a life of rural poverty. From the beginning people
started to recognize that young Oprah would be different. Oprah
demonstrated her early intelligence by learning to read by the age of
three. She also had the uncanny ability to memorize a large number of
bible verses. Her ability was so astounding she was nicknamed "the
Preacher" by members of the local congregation.

Despite her abilities, life remained hard for young Oprah. Winfrey and
her mother ended up moving to inner city Milwaukee, Wisconsin when
she was six years old. It is said that Oprah's mother was not very
supportive of her daughter. Oprah was even molested by family
members when she was nine. These events led to Oprah rebelling
against her mother, running away from home, and becoming pregnant at
the age of 14. Tragically her baby died shortly after its birth. At that
point Oprah's mother sent her away to live with her father in Nashville,
Tennessee. It was in Nashville that Oprah bloomed, becoming a top
student, speech team member, and popular among her classmates.
Because of her speaking skills she was awarded a full scholarship to
attend Tennessee State University (TSU), a historically black college in
Nashville.

Her time at TSU was very productive as she excelled in the classroom while majoring in communications. It was during her time at TSU that Oprah won the title of "Miss Black Tennessee". Oprah also worked at a local radio station during her college years. Oprah began her news career at WLAC-TV becoming the station's youngest and first black female news anchor. In 1976, Oprah moved to Baltimore to become co-anchor of the 6:00 news, as well as the co-host of her first talk show, *People are Talking*.

In 1983, Oprah was invited to be the host of a Chicago talk show called *A.M. Chicago*. *A.M. Chicago* had the dubious distinction of being the lowest rated Chicago talk-show at the time. Amazingly, after just a few months with Oprah as the host, the show was #1 in Chicago, even beating out the mega-hit show *Donahue*. With this local success the show was expanded and sent out nationally in 1986. Quickly the show became #1 replacing *Donahue* as the top talk-show in all of America.

Over the years the show has evolved from a tabloid-style talk-show to a higher brow show. Most of the topics featured on *The Oprah Winfrey Show* today focus on issues of disease, spirituality, religion, substance abuse, and literature. Some of the more popular developments from *The Oprah Winfrey Show* have been: *Oprah's Book Club*, *Pay it Forward*, and the *Dr. Phil Show*. Oprah Winfrey has truly cemented her reputation for being America's foremost TV interviewer. Oprah was even the host of a prime-time interview with Michael Jackson in 1993. That interview became the 4th most watched television event in history.

In addition to being America's favorite talk show host, Oprah has many other professional accomplishments. Oprah is a prize winning author, publisher, radio host, and actor. Oprah's most famous role occurred in the move *The Color Purple*. Oprah's *O Magazine* has the distinction of being the most successful magazine start up in history. Oprah currently heads the satellite radio channel *Oprah & Friends*, which broadcasts shows by hand picked experts 24 hours per day 7 days per week.

The Oprah Winfrey Show has been broadcast for so many years, and is so popular, getting tickets can be a bit tricky. The show currently films about 140 shows per year, filming 2 shows per day, which means the Oprah show only films on 70 days per year. The episode filming runs from September to early December and then resumes in January running to early June. In order to get tickets guests must call the reservation line from 9:00 a.m. until 5:00 p.m. Reservations can be made up to one month in advance. Unfortunately, the topic for the show is not released until the day of the show, and callers generally will not have a choice between which session they can attend. The worst time to try to make a reservation is right after the show airs. The best time to call is between 1:30 p.m. and 3:00 p.m. Guests are allowed to attend one taping every six weeks (although it is suggested guests only attend once per season), and guests generally must be 18+ (ID's will be checked at the door).

Chicagoland Fun Fact

One of most famous celebrities in the history of Chicago is George Wendt. Wendt is known nationally for his role as Norm Peterson in the long running hit show *Cheers*. Wendt is most loved by Chicagoans for his recurring guest role on Saturday Night Live as Chicago Superfan Bob Swerski, as well as his character's catchphrase "Da Bears"!

Chicago Greeter Service

77 East Randolph Street

Chicago, IL 60602

312-744-8000

www.chicagogreeter.com

Free Admission Days: Always Free

As part of its dedication to its visitors, the city of Chicago offers one of the most unique services in the country. The free Chicago Greeter Program was enacted in 2001 in an effort to familiarize visitors with the sights, sounds, flavors, and accessibility of the city. The program consists of an army of well trained volunteers who are able to guide visitors around the city, via walking and public transportation. The program whisks visitors around all corners of the city, pointing out fine museums, shops, and eating establishments. Each tour can range from two to four hours, and each tour has a set theme. Tour guides are often residents of the areas they guide visitors, thus are a great resource for inside information about fun things to do in each neighborhood. Catering to tourists from all over the world, the tours are offered in over 20 different languages. The tours are free to visitors, but must be booked at least seven days in advance.

For visitors who are just popping into the city on a whim, Chicago also offers the InstaGreeter service. The InstaGreeter service offers walking tours which concentrate on the downtown Chicago area. The InstaGreeter tour lasts about an hour and details Chicago's rich history, as well as hot visitor spots. The InstaGreeter service is available Friday, Saturday, and Sunday from 10:00 a.m. until 4:00 p.m., and is offered on a first come first served basis.

APPENDIX

Traveling around Chicago

Being the third largest city in the U.S., traveling the streets of Chicago can be a bit daunting to the average visitor. One major obstacle to traveling around Chicago is parking. Unfortunately there are many cases where a free attraction can become unaffordable simply because of the cost of parking a car nearby. It is always a good idea to call ahead to any attraction to see what the best parking strategies are. Fortunately, most all of the workers at an attraction are local so they will be able to give you the best (and often cheapest) options.

One strategy that is highly recommended is to take advantage of the public transportation system of Chicago. The Chicago Transit Authority (CTA) is in charge of the bus and train network which shuttles citizens and visitors around the "Windy City". The CTA is made up of over 2,000 busses and 1,000 train cars which combine to move over 1.6 million riders per day. The CTA's network of routs is so large that it is made up of over 2,500 route miles.

For visitors, the CTA offers several affordable options. The best option for most visitors is the Visitor's Pass. The Visitor's Pass grants the user unlimited trips aboard the trains and busses of the CTA. Passes are available for periods of one day up to five days. The great thing about the pass is the fact that the card's time doesn't start until it is punched the first time, thus visitors who get the one day pass get a full 24 hours of unlimited riding. Riders over 7 years of age would be well served with the Visitor's Pass. The CTA always allows riders age 7 or under to ride for free.

Visitors who take advantage of the convenient public transit system will also get a good value for parking. A good strategy for parking in the city is to use the parking lots of the Park and Ride system. About $2.00 grants the visitor up to 24 hours of parking time at one of 18 different locations. Parking at the CTA stations can result in major savings as it is not unheard of to have to pay $15 per day for downtown lots. With some planning ahead, and a visit to the CTA's web-site, (www.transitchicago.com) much expense and aggravation can be avoided.

Important Web Sites and Phone Numbers

Chicago Convention and Tourism Bureau

2301 South Lake Shore Drive
Chicago, IL 60616
Phone: 312-567-8500

www.choosechicago.com

Chicago Transit Authority

567 West Lake Street
Chicago, IL 60661
Phone: 312-681-3094

www.transitchicago.com

City of Chicago Government

2111 West Lexington
Chicago, IL 60612
Phone: 312-744-3500

www.cityofchicago.org

Chicagoland Regional Tourism Development Office

2301 South Lakeshore Drive
Chicago, IL 60616
Phone: 312-795-1700

www.chicagolandtravel.com

Illinois Bureau of Tourism

100 West Randolph, Suite 3-400
Chicago, IL 60601
Phone: 312-814-4733

www.enjoyillinois.com

Photos Used In the Book

Cover and Introduction
John Hancock Building as seen from Chicago Avenue

Science and Industry
Adler Planetarium

History Museums
Gargoyle at the Cobb entrance of the University of Chicago

Historical Sites
Old Chicago Water Tower

Religious Sites
Baha'i Temple located in Wilmette

Art Galleries and Museums
Bronze Lion outside the Art Institute of Chicago

Nature Days
View from inside the Lincoln Park Conservatory

Uniquely Chicagoland
View of an "L" railcar

Appendix
Interstate highway sign

Printed in the United States
118963LV00003B/66/P